The United States Marines in the Civil War:
Harpers Ferry and the Battle of First Manassas

Major Bruce H. "Doc" Norton, USMC (Ret)
&
Master Sergeant Phillip Gibbons, USMC (Ret)

With map illustrations by
Mr. Brian D. Wishner

The United States Marines in the Civil War:
Harpers Ferry and the Battle of First Manassas

Major Bruce H. "Doc" Norton, USMC (Ret)
&
Master Sergeant Phillip Gibbons, USMC (Ret)

With map illustrations by
Mr. Brian D. Wishner

Academica Press
Washington - London

Library of Congress Cataloging-in-Publication Data

Names: Norton, Bruce H. (author) | Gibbons, Phillip (author)
Title: The united states marines in the civil war : harpers ferry and the
battle of first manassas | Bruce H. Norton and Phillip Gibbons
Description: Washington : Academica Press, 2021. | Includes references.
Identifiers: LCCN 2021931617 | ISBN 9781680539578 (hardcover) |
ISBN 9781680538151 (paperback) | ISBN 9781680538168 (e-book)

ACKNOWLEDGMENTS

I want to thank my wife Helen, who listened to the many great stories that came from the writing of this book.

My sincere thanks to my friend Lieutenant General George "Ron" Christmas, USMC (Ret), who described his personal involvement with the story of Private Luke Quinn, USMC, the only Marine killed during the capture of John Brown.

My thanks to Dr. Paul du Quenoy, President and Publisher of Academica Press, and a fellow historian. Thank you, Paul, for making this possible.

Our thanks to the excellent editing done by the staff at Academica Press. Thank you for making us look good on paper.

To my coworkers at the Lejeune Leadership Institute: Colonel Seth Ocloo, USMC, Dr. James I. Van Zummeren, USMC (Ret.), Lieutenant Colonel Mathew J. Keller, USMC, and Major Greg Dyson, USMC, who read several draft copies of this book and provided valuable comments to make it only better.

My sincere thanks to Dr. Edward T. Nevgloski, the Director of the Marine Corps' History Division at Marine Corps University, for permissions, access, guidance, and encouragement to tell the story of our Corps.

Our sincere thanks to Mr. Dan Chitchester, Mr. Paul Scott, and Mr. Chip Willis, who offered valuable criticisms, comments, and corrections to help make this book a valuable contribution to our Corps' history.

Our sincere thanks to Mr. Brain D. "Crayola" Wishner, who brought the movement of the Marine Battalion to life on the Manassas Battlefield with his rendering of such great maps.

As it "takes a village to raise a child," it takes a great number of people, working behind the scenes, to write, delineate, proof-read, edit, and publish a book. My sincere thanks to everyone who helped Phillip Gibbons and me to accomplish this task.

-- Major Bruce H. "Doc" Norton, USMC (Ret)

I will begin by thanking my wife Betty and our daughter Saralynn, who maintained our small farm, taking care of sick horses, dealing with downed trees on the pasture fence, enduring snowstorms and a host of other issues, while I was off conducting research, or at the Manassas Battlefield with Doc. Thank you so very much, ladies!

Additionally, there are many other individuals who deserve my sincere thanks for their assistance in the researching and writing of this book. The Director of the United States Marine Corps Historical Company, Gunnery Sergeant Tom Williams, USMC (Ret), for his selfless support of this project. Tom has spent countless hours with me researching the Marine's actions at Harpers Ferry and at the Battle of 1st Manassas (Bull Run), beginning in 2003. He welcomed me into his home and granted me free access to all of his research materials, artifacts, and the numerous articles he has written about the nineteenth-century Marine Corps. Tom provided mentoring and guidance during the many hours spent walking on the Manassas Battlefield.

I wish to thank Dr. Charlie P. Neimeyer and Dr. Edward T. Nevgloski, the former and current Directors of the Marine Corps History Division at Quantico, Virginia. These two men, both Marine Corps officers and historians, have inspired me over the years to ensure that the story of our Corps was accurately told.

My sincere thanks to fellow author "Gunner" Will Hutchinson for his sharing of writing experience and mostly his wonderful sense of humor.

My gratitude to the staff at Manassas National Battlefield Park who have been fantastic with their support during our multiple visits to that hallowed ground.

My sincere thanks to Dr. Paul du Quenoy, our publisher, who knew that we had a story worthy of Academica Press.

And, last but certainly not least, my thanks to my coauthor, Major Bruce H. "Doc" Norton, USMC (Ret), for without Doc, I am sure this book would never have been published. Doc's great historical knowledge, friendship and patience, and his experience as an author has kept me on track in getting my deliverable materials to him for his review and editing. Thank you, all!

-- Phillip Gibbons

Contents

INTRODUCTION

The world of writing military history is filled with truths, half-truths, gross exaggerations, and absolute lies (today referred to as "misinformation"). The purpose of this book was to correct the latter of the three, to present the most accurate picture of what the United States Marine Corps looked like in 1861, and to describe the actions of the battalion of Marines present at the Battle of First Manassas, or as the Union liked to call it, Bull Run.[1]

The United States Marine Corps has a colorful 245-year history replete with adventures and acts of heroism performed by brave young men and women. Throughout the years, though, many of their stories, handed down from generation to generation, have been told within the confines of boot camp squad bays, and during dining-in and mess night gatherings held throughout our Corps.

Along the way, however, many important details have been omitted, others greatly embellished, and in some cases, many created only to make a great "war story" that much more colorful and interesting. In the case of the United States Marines' actions at the Battle of First Manassas, on Sunday, July 21, 1861, the complete story has not been accurately told for many generations. Their actions at the Battle of 1st Manassas have been unnecessarily criticized and the excuses for these actions often explained as: "Well, they were all just raw recruits..." or, "the Marines were not as an effective force in the middle of the nineteenth century as they are today." Both statements are inaccurate, and to Marines, insulting.

Since 1775, Continental Marines manned the rigging of US Navy ships and have distinguished themselves in a number of important amphibious

---

[1] American Civil War battles often had one name in the North which was usually associated with a prominent nearby physical feature, and another in the South which was usually derived from the town of city closest to the battlefield. The strategic significance of the location lay in the fact that Manassas was an important railroad junction.

operations, including their first amphibious raid, in the Bahamas in March 1776 under the command of Capt. (later Maj.) Samuel Nicholas. The first commissioned officer in the Continental Marines, Nicholas remained the senior Marine officer throughout the American Revolution and today is recognized as the first Marine Commandant.

The Treaty of Paris, in April 1783, brought an end to the Revolutionary War, and as the last of the Navy's ships were sold, the Continental Navy and Marines went out of existence. Following the Revolutionary War and the formal re-establishment of the Marine Corps on 11 July 1798, the Marines saw action in the quasi-war with France, landed in Santo Domingo, and took part in many operations against the Barbary pirates along the "Shores of Tripoli." Marines also took part in numerous naval operations during the War of 1812, as well as participating in the defense of Washington, D.C., at Bladensburg, Maryland, and fought alongside Andrew Jackson in his victory over the British at New Orleans, Louisiana.

The decades following the War of 1812 saw Marines protecting American interests around the world, in the Caribbean, the Falkland Islands, the Mediterranean, and also close to home in operations against the Seminole Indians in the western swamps of Florida. Marines have participated in all subsequent American wars, and in most cases were the first service members to fight. By 1859, the Marines were a well-established professional force in readiness.

To tell the story of the actions of U.S. Marines in the Manassas Campaign, we begin this book with their actions at Harpers Ferry. The Marines were the only professional fighting force that could respond immediately when the call for assistance came to address the situation at the Federal Armory. These Marines were led by professional, well-trained officers and non-commissioned officers, who continued a standard that existed prior to 1859, that Marines were "at all times ready" – and our Corps remains so to this very day.

Having reviewed numerous military history books, studied national and local archives, read voluminous personal correspondence, official reports and newspaper clippings, and examined photographs and inaccurate maps, Master Sergeant Philip Gibbons, USMC (Ret), and I agreed that we were not comfortable with previous accounts of the actions of United States

Marines at the 1st Battle of Manassas. We have attempted here to describe what actually happened, and with new and detailed maps illustrated by Mr. Brian P. Wishner, the movement of the Marine Battalion is, for the first time, accurately depicted in a clear and detailed sequence leading up to and throughout Sunday, July 21, 1861.

- Major Bruce H. "Doc" Norton, USMC (Ret)

CHAPTER 1

The United States Marines and John Brown's Raid

On July 3, 1859, John Brown arrived in Harpers Ferry, 61 miles northwest of Washington, DC, in what was then the Commonwealth of Virginia (now, West Virginia), accompanied by his two sons, Oliver and Owen, and Jeremiah Anderson. In the preceding months, he had raised money from other abolitionists and ordered pikes, guns, and other weapons to be used in his war against slavery. Using the alias Isaac Smith, Brown rented the Kennedy Farm, located about five miles from the Federal Armory, on the Maryland side of the Potomac River.

Throughout the summer Brown's Army gathered at the farmhouse. Numbering 21 at the time of the raid, these men stayed hidden in the attic by day, reading, writing letters, polishing their rifles, and playing checkers. To avoid being seen by curious neighbors, they would only come out at night.

(John Brown – 1859)

To keep up the appearance of a normal household, Brown sent for his daughter, 15-year-old Annie, and Oliver's wife, 17-year-old Martha. The girls prepared meals, washed clothes, and kept nosy neighbors at a distance. Brown studied maps and conferred with John Cook, his advance man in the Ferry, about the town, armory operations, train schedules, and other information deemed valuable to his plan. On September 30, Brown sent Martha and Annie home to New York. The time was near.

(Annie Brown - John Brown's Daughter)

(Martha Brown, John Brown's Daughter-in-Law)

On Sunday, October 16, Brown called his men together. Following a prayer, he outlined his battle plans and instructed them, "Men, get your arms; we will proceed to the Ferry."

"Harpers Ferry was the site of a major federal armory, including a musket factory and rifle works, an arsenal, several large mills and an important railroad junction and was one of the most heavily industrialized towns south of the Mason-Dixon line," said Dennis Frye, the National Park Service's Chief Historian at Harpers Ferry. "It was also a cosmopolitan town, with a lot of Irish and German immigrants, and even Yankees who worked in the industrial facilities." The town and its environs' population of 3,000 included about 300 African Americans evenly divided between slave and free. But more than 18,000 slaves – the "bees" Brown expected to swarm – lived in the surrounding counties.

The Military Responds

In 1859, James Ewell Brown Stuart, was a 1st Lieutenant in the U.S. Cavalry, enjoying six months' leave from his frontier post at Fort Riley, Kansas Territory. Yet the joys of coming home to Virginia had not made him forget he was a cavalryman by profession. On the rainy morning of October 17, he had ridden over the muddy streets of Washington to the offices of the War Department, and now sat waiting to speak with the Secretary of War, John B. Floyd.

J. E. B. Stuart had invented and patented an improved device that attached a cavalryman's sabre to his belt, and he was attempting to sell the patent to the War Department. On that Monday morning, he was waiting for an interview in the anteroom of the Secretary.[1] While the young lieutenant was rehearsing in his mind for the coming interview, the Secretary himself was face to face with the specter of a slave insurrection.

**((Top)1st Lieutenant J. E. B. Stuart, U.S. Army Cavalry –
(Bottom) Stuart's letter to the Adjutant General, War Department
referencing the "Stuarts' Sabre Attachment")**

John B. Floyd was a poor administrator, a failing which almost resulted in his removal from office; but on this day there was no time for paper shuffling. Word had come by way of Baltimore that "an insurrection had broken out at Harpers Ferry and a band of armed men had captured the United States arsenal there and was forming a slave rebellion." A native of Virginia, the Secretary must have heard of the often-told tales of the Haitians' revolt against their French masters with all its barbarism. Nor had any son of the Old Dominion forgotten Nat Turner's Rebellion, a slave uprising which occurred a generation before and claimed the lives of 55 whites in a single bloody night.

(Captain Edward O. C. Ord, U.S. Army)

Swinging into action, Floyd fired off a telegram to Fort Monroe; by noon Captain Edward O. C. Ord and 150 artillerymen were on their way toward Baltimore on the first leg of the journey to Harpers Ferry. There was no question as to who would command operations against the insurgents. Floyd called for his chief clerk and set him to writing orders summoning to the War Department Brevet Colonel Robert E. Lee, then on leave at his estate, Arlington, just across the Potomac River from the capital.

(Brevet Colonel Robert E, Lee, U.S. Army – 1859)

Message in hand, the harassed aide came dashing out of the office, only to halt when he spied the forgotten cavalry officer. J. E. B. Stuart, by now thoroughly bored, and had easily persuaded him to deliver the sealed envelope. Even as this message was speeding toward its destination, President James Buchanan called Secretary Floyd to move even faster, a demand which was to bring the Marine Corps into the picture.

Since there were no troops nearer the scene of the uprising than those en route from Fort Monroe, Floyd was powerless to comply; but Secretary of the Navy Isaac Toucey quickly offered a solution to the dilemma. About noon, Charles W. Welsh, chief clerk of the Navy Department, came riding through the main gate of the Washington Navy Yard. He sought out First Lieutenant Israel Greene, the Officer-of-the Day, and temporarily in command of Marine Barracks, Washington, and asked how many leathernecks were available for duty.

(1st Lieutenant Israel Greene – 1859)

Lieutenant Greene estimated that he could round up some 86 men from both his barracks and the small Navy yard detachment. He then asked Welsh what was wrong. The civilian told him all he knew – that the armory at Harpers Ferry had been seized by a group of abolitionists, and that state and federal troops were already on the march. As a "line officer," 1st Lieutenant Greene was allowed by law to lead Marines in combat.

As the senior line officer on duty at the Navy Yard, 1st Lieutenant Greene assumed the burden of organizing the expedition. Major William W. Russell, Paymaster of the Corps, was detailed to assist him; but Russell, a staff officer, could not exercise command over the force. Major Russell was an experienced line officer from his time fighting in the Mexican War and his expertise could be depended upon if necessary. Colonel John Harris, Commandant of the Marine Corps, also felt the presence of a more mature person was required. Greene, after all had only a dozen years' service to his credit, and Russell's presence might prevent unnecessary bloodshed. Working with the major, Greene, saw to it that each of his six sergeants and 80 other Marines had drawn muskets, ball cartridges, and rations.

Since no one knew for certain the strength or exact position of the insurgent force, two 12-pound Dahlgren heavy boat howitzers and several shrapnel shells were made ready. At 15:30, the Leathernecks clambered aboard a Baltimore and Ohio train and rattled off toward Harpers Ferry.

(12-Pound Dahlgren Howitzer – 1858)

(Secretary of the Navy Isaac Toucey – 1859)

Mr. Welsh reported back to the Navy Department and Secretary Toucey and at once began drafting an order to Colonel Harris. "Send all the available Marines at Headquarters," he wrote, "under charge of suitable officers by this evening's train of cars to Harpers Ferry to protect the public property at that place, which is endangered by a riotous outbreak." Once they arrive at their destination, the Leathernecks would be under the command of the senior U.S. Army officer present, in this case Colonel Robert E. Lee.

While Secretary Toucey was busy alerting the Marines, J. E. B. Stuart had returned from Arlington with Colonel Lee. Once again, the lieutenant waited in the Secretary's anteroom as Floyd outlined the crisis to Lee. There was no need to stress the savage implications of a slave uprising, for the colonel had been stationed at Fort Monroe when Nat Turner had put aside his plough to take up the sword, and he well remembered the terror that followed. He recalled, too, how militia, regulars, and Marines from Norfolk had scoured the Virginia countryside before bringing Nat Turner to bay deep in the vastness of Dismal Swamp. After receiving the latest intelligence from western Virginia, Lee was handed orders placing him in overall command of the effort to suppress the insurrection.

Accompanied by Stuart, Floyd and Lee hurried to the White House, where the colonel was given a proclamation of martial law to issue if he should see fit. In addition to the proclamation, Lee acquired an aide. Certain that a fight of some sort was at hand, Stuart volunteered to accompany him to Harpers Ferry, and Lee accepted. Still in civilian clothes the colonel hurried to the railroad station, but the Marines had already left.

The next train to leave the National Capital was the Baltimore Express. At 17:00, Lee and Stuart boarded the train in the hope of catching up with the column at Relay House, a railroad station near Baltimore where the Marines had to change trains. They were, again, too late, and the expedition rolled off toward its goal without its commanding officer. Lee then wired the stationmaster at Sandy Hook, Maryland, to hold the trainload of Leathernecks until he and his aide arrived. For the time being, all the two officers could do was wait. Fortunately, they were not delayed for long. John W. Garrett, president of the Baltimore and Ohio Railroad, learned of Lee's plight and ordered a locomotive to Relay House. Aware that a few moments wasted might cost him his job, the engineer opened wide the throttle. At 22:00, Lee arrived at Sandy Hook on the Maryland side of the Potomac River across the bridge from Harpers Ferry. Major

Russell and Lieutenant Greene were waiting as the Army officers descended from the cab. Lee now learned the details of the insurrection.

It had happened so quickly. On the night of October 17, at about 22:30, eighteen armed men were led by a farmer who called himself Isaac Smith. (Some said he was called "Old Osawatomie"). John Brown of Kansas padded across the covered, wooden railroad trestle leading into the town and made a prisoner of one of the bridge tenders. Next, the raiders strolled through the darkness and up to the gates of the United States armory. They leveled their pistols at a startled watchman and quickly gained access to the buildings.

The leader of the band then sent out patrols to take hostages. Most prominent among the captives was Lewis W. Washington, a colonel on the staff of Governor Henry A. Wise of Virginia and a great-grandnephew of George Washington. His captors forced him to hand over a sword given to the first President of the United States by Frederick the Great of Prussia, and a pistol given to the President by the Marquis de Lafayette in 1778. During the nightmare that followed, this sword and pistol hung at the side of the man who called himself Smith. (See Appendix 1)

(Lewis W. Washington – 1858)

While the prisoners were being rounded up, the second bridge tender, Mr. Patrick Higgins, wandered out onto the span in search of his partner. In the darkness, he collided with two of the raiders who had been posted as guards. A single punch floored one of them, and as the other fired wildly Higgins sprinted back to the town. The angry, red crease etched lightly across his scalp by a rifle bullet was proof enough that Harpers Ferry was under attack.

The raiders next showed their hand when the eastbound night express neared Harpers Ferry. Afraid the bridge had been weakened, a railroad employee flagged the train to a halt short of the trestle. A party of trainmen walked out onto the span to investigate but were driven back by a volley of rifle fire. Mortally wounded by the self-appointed liberators was Shepard Hayward, a freed slave. Until dawn, the raiders held the train at Harpers Ferry. Then the locomotive gingerly eased its cars across the bridge, gathered momentum, and roared off toward Frederick, Maryland. There, it halted while the conductor wired a garbled report of the insurrection to the railroad's main office in Baltimore. This news was relayed to the governors of Maryland and Virginia; militiamen were alerted and sent marching toward the embattled town. Next, a telegram was dispatched to the Secretary of War, and now, at last, Colonel Lee and the Marines arrived on scene.[2]

"At All Times Ready" – U.S. Marine Actions at Harpers Ferry

October 16, 2020, marked 161 years since John Brown perpetrated his raid against the Federal Armory and the town of Harpers Ferry, Virginia. Today, we can find little fault with John Brown's motivation, but controversy still rages as to his methods. Although Brown's raid made an indelible mark on our nation's history, many of the details and the people involved are still shrouded in myth and conjecture.

Few people today realize that U.S. Marines captured John Brown, ending his attempt to incite a slave revolt in Virginia and the surrounding area. Fewer still grasp either the military and political intrigue beyond the issue of slavery that surrounded the raid or the challenges Army Colonel Robert E. Lee, and the Marines he commanded, would face in resolving the issue.

Their ability to improvise and adapt to the rapidly changing mission, and the courage and discipline that ultimately allowed them to defuse a very tense and explosive situation, would directly reflect upon those operations that Marines deal with around the world today.

(Harpers Ferry Engine-House – 1860)

Early reports claimed that Harpers Ferry had been taken by 50, then 150, then 200 white "insurrectionists" and "six hundred runaway negroes." John Brown expected to have 1,500 men under his command by midday Monday. He later said he believed he would eventually have armed as many as 5,000 slaves. But the bees did not swarm. Only a handful of slaves lent Brown assistance. Instead, as Brown's band watched dawn break over the craggy ridges enclosing Harpers Ferry, local white militiamen – like today's National Guard – were hastening to arms.

First to arrive were the Jefferson Guards from nearby Charles Town. Uniformed in blue with tall black hats on their heads and brandishing muskets, they seized the railway bridge, killing a former slave named Dangerfield Newby and cutting John Brown off from his escape route.

Newby had gone north in a failed attempt to earn enough money to buy freedom for his wife and six children. In his pocket was a letter from his wife: "It is said Master is in want of money," she had written. "I know not what time he may sell me, and then all my bright hopes of the future are blasted, for their [*sic*] has been one bright hope to cheer me in all my troubles, that is to be with you."[3]

As the day progressed, armed units poured in from Frederick, Maryland, Martinsburg and Shepherdstown, Virginia, and elsewhere. Brown and his raiders were soon surrounded. He and a dozen of his men held out in the engine house, a small but formidable brick building with stout oak doors in front. Other small groups remained holed up in the musket factory and rifle works. Acknowledging their increasingly dire predicament, Brown sent out New Yorker William Thompson, bearing a white flag, to propose a cease-fire. But Thompson was captured and held in the Galt House, a local hotel. Brown then dispatched his son, Watson, and ex-cavalryman Aaron Stevens, also under a white flag, but the militiamen shot them down in the street. Watson, though fatally wounded, managed to crawl back to the engine house. Stevens, shot four times, was then arrested.

When militia units from Maryland and Virginia converged on the scene, Brown and five of his remaining men, four still unwounded and able to fire their rifle, along with eleven hostages, were cornered in the arsenal's fire-engine house. The fifth raider, Brown's son Oliver, lay mortally wounded and unable to take any further action.

[Of the three sons of John Brown who participated in the Harpers Ferry attack, Watson (left) was mortally wounded, as was Oliver (middle). Owen (right) managed to escape. (Library of Congress)]

During the night, Colonel Lee led his small force of U.S. Marines across the railroad bridge and into the town. Lee sized up the situation to avoid further bloodshed, especially among the hostages, and quickly but quietly, had the Marines relieve the militiamen guarding the perimeter of the Federal Armory. Dealing with difficult conditions, Lee waited for more daylight before acting. Because this was still considered a "local" matter, he offered the mission of attacking the firehouse to both state militias, but their leaders declined his offer. A Virginia colonel is reputed to have remarked: "You are paid for doing this kind of work."

Rescuing the hostages now fell to the Marines. Lieutenant Greene eagerly accepted the job and began planning the assault. The storming party would consist of Greene and twelve Marines, with an additional two Marines armed with sledgehammers to help break down the Armory's door. Another twelve Marines would stand in reserve. Lee feared that in the dim light of dawn, distinguishing friend from foe would be difficult and the chances of hostages being injured by "friendly fire" too great. He ordered the Marines to make the assault with muskets unloaded and to rely solely on their bayonets. At daylight, Stuart was to deliver a note from Lee to the leader of the insurrection force demanding his surrender. If the insurgent refused, Stuart was to wave his hat, signaling the Marines to launch an immediate assault.

(One of the sledgehammer heads used to break down the door of the
Harpers Ferry Engine House – on display at the
National Museum of the Marine Corps.)

At dawn, following a night of light rain, Stuart made the final attempt to obtain a peaceful end to the affair. At that time, the federal forces were still unsure who was the actual head of the raiders. Although going by the name of Isaac Smith, rumors were spreading that it was, in fact, "Old Osawatomie," John Brown of Kansas fame. When Brown received the note, he attempted to negotiate with Stuart. As ordered, the Cavalry officer would have no part of it and made his signal.

The Marines rushed forward. When the sledgehammers proved incapable of doing the job against the Armory's sturdy wooden doors, Lieutenant Greene ordered his men to grab a nearby heavy ladder. Two blows from this makeshift battering ram in the upper door hinge broke causing the door to pivot inward and created a triangular opening. This was because heavy ropes had been tied across the door's opening by Brown's men, preventing an easy breach.

The lieutenant was the first man through, followed by Major Russell, reportedly, carrying only a rattan switch. Behind them the Marines "came rushing in like tigers." The first figure Greene encountered as he rushed in was Lewis Washington, one of the hostages and an acquaintance of the lieutenant. He quickly pointed out John Brown.

Lieutenant Greene attacked Brown, but his initial sword thrust struck the heavy leather belt that Brown was wearing across his chest, bending the blade of Greene's sword, and, though disabling Brown, it failed to kill him. Greene continued to attack Brown and beat him senseless with his useless sword. Private Luke Quinn, while attempting to break down the door, was shot in the groin and died of his wound soon after. Private Matthew Ruppert was shot through the cheek but would recover. Seeing that the remaining insurrectionists had surrendered, Greene called a halt to the onslaught. The entire action was over in less than three minutes.

A correspondent of the *Richmond Daily Dispatch*, who was an eyewitness to the assault would report: "Immediately the signal for the attack was given, and the Marines... advanced in two lines on each side of the door. Two powerful fellows sprang between the lines, and with heavy sledgehammers attempted to batter down the door. The door swung and swayed, but appeared to be secured with a rope, the spring of which deadened the effect of the sledgehammer blows. Failing thus to obtain a breach, the Marines were ordered to fall back, and a [dozen] of them took hold of a ladder, some [twenty feet] long, and advancing at a run, brought it with tremendous power against the door. At the second blow it gave way, one leaf falling inward in a slanting position. The Marines immediately advanced to the breach, Major Russell and Lieutenant Greene leading the way. A Marine in front fell; the firing from the interior was rapid and sharp, they fired with deliberate aim, and for the moment the resistance is serious and desperate enough to excite the spectators to something like a pitched frenzy. The next moment the Marines pour in, the firing ceases and the work was done, whilst the cheers rang from every side, the general feeling being that the Marines had done their part admirably."

After freeing the hostages, the Marines, led by Drum Major John Roach of the Marine Band, removed Brown, who had been wounded in the neck by Greene's saber blow, along with two other surviving raiders from the engine house. They now had to assume the job of safeguarding the men they had just captured from an angry lynch mob.

The Marines retained control of the prisoners, holding them in a house located across the street from the Federal Armory. Four hours after the assault, Private Quinn died of his wounds in the room next to where John Brown was being interrogated by Colonel Lee and Lieutenant Greene. The Marines escorted John Brown and his fellow conspirators to Charlestown, Virginia, at about noon on the October 19, and turned the conspirators over to civilian authorities for incarceration and trial. That evening, the Marines were sent to Pleasant Valley, Maryland, following a rumor of further insurrection. These rumors proved to be false, and the Marines returned to Washington on October 20.

John Brown was hastily tried for treason against the Commonwealth of Virginia, the murder of five men, and inciting a slave insurrection. Upon hearing his death sentence, Brown said: "if it is deemed necessary that I should forfeit my life for the furtherance of the ends of justice, and mingle my blood further with the blood of my children and with the blood of millions in this slave country whose rights are disregarded by wicked, cruel, and unjust enactments – I submit; so let it be done!" Brown told the court he had hoped to carry out his plans "without the snapping of a gun on either side." But Brown's vision of ending slavery was marred by the deaths of innocent civilians – both in Kansas and at Harpers Ferry. The nation was divided over his actions. Many abolitionists called him a hero. Slaveholders called him a base villain. People on both sides of the fence denounced Brown's use of violence.

John Brown was hanged on December 2, 1859. Before he died, he issued these final, seemingly prophetic words in a note he handed to his jailer: "Charlestown, VA, 2nd December, 1859, I John Brown am now quite certain that the crimes of this guilty land will never be purged away but with Blood. I had as I now think vainly flattered myself that without very much bloodshed; it might be done." He was the first person executed for treason in the history of the country. Just over a year later, the first Southern state would secede from the Union.[4]

Colonel Robert E. Lee officially praised the United States Marines in his report writing of "the conduct of the detachment of Marines, who were at all times ready and prompt in the execution of any duty." Lee sent a personal note to Marine Corps Commandant John Harris, commenting: "Your Corps has captivated so many hearts in Virginia."

"Had John Brown's raid not occurred, it is very possible that the 1860 election would have been a regular two-party contest between anti-slavery Republicans and pro-slavery Democrats," says City University of New York historian David Reynolds, author of *John Brown: Abolitionist.* "The Democrats would probably have won, since Abraham Lincoln received just 40 percent of the popular vote, around one million votes less than his three opponents." While the Democrats split over slavery, Republican candidates such as William Seward were tarnished by their association with abolitionists; Lincoln, at the time, was regarded as one of his party's more conservative options. "John Brown was, in effect, a hammer that shattered Lincoln's opponents into fragments," says Reynolds. "Because Brown helped to disrupt the party system, Lincoln was carried to victory, which in turn led 11 states to secede from the Union. This in turn led to the Civil War."[5]

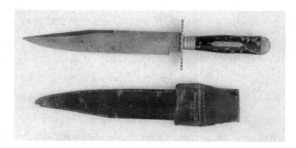

This photograph shows John Brown's bowie knife, manufactured in Sheffield, England, by G. Wostenholm & Son, and features a tortoise-shell handle and a steel blade marked with the identification "The Real I *XL Knife/The Hunter's Companion." Lt. J. E. B. Stuart claimed to have taken this knife during the John Brown's failed attack on the Federal Armory at Harpers Ferry, Virginia, on October 16, 1859. In a January 1860 letter to his mother, Elizabeth Letcher Stuart, Stuart boasted that he "immediately recognized Old Ossawatomie Brown, who had given us so much trouble ... in Kansas, and that he took Brown's bowie knife as a souvenir."

The following extracts are taken from a letter which Stuart wrote to his mother from Fort Riley, Kansas, in January 1860. Several contemporary newspaper accounts gave him the credit for having led the attack upon the engine house in which John Brown had taken refuge, an honor which Stuart was careful to disclaim. (The letter is transcribed from H. B. McClellan, *Life and Campaigns of J. E. B. Stuart*, Boston, 1885, pp. 28-30):

> *Colonel Lee was sent to command the forces at Harpers Ferry. I volunteered as his aid. I had no command whatever. The United States marines are a branch of the naval force, – there was not an enlisted man of the army on hand. Lieutenant Greene was sent in command. Major Russell had been requested by the Secretary of the Navy to accompany the marines, but, being a paymaster, could exercise no command; yet it was his corps. For Colonel Lee to have put me in command of the storming party would have been an outrage to Lieutenant Greene, which would have rung through the navy for twenty years. As well might they send him out here to command my company of cavalry ....*

I, too, had a part to perform, which prevented me in a measure from participating in the very brief onset made so gallantly by Greene and Russell, well backed by their men. I was deputed by Colonel Lee to read to the leader, then called Smith, a demand to surrender immediately; and I was instructed to leave the door after his refusal, which was expected, and wave my cap; at which signal the storming party was to advance, batter open the doors, and capture the insurgents at the point of the bayonet. Colonel Lee cautioned the stormers particularly to discriminate between the insurgents and their prisoners.

I approached the door in the presence of perhaps two thousand spectators and told Mr. Smith that I had a communication for him from Colonel Lee. He opened the door about four inches, and placed his body against the crack, with a cocked carbine in his hand: hence his remark after his capture that he could have wiped me out like a mosquito. The parley was a long one. He presented his propositions in every possible shape, and with admirable tact; but all amounted to this: that the only condition upon which he would surrender was that he and his party should be allowed to escape. Some of his prisoners begged me to ask Colonel Lee to come and see him. I told them he would never accede to any terms but those he had offered; and as soon as I could tear myself away from their importunities, I left the door and waved my cap, and Colonel Lee's plan was carried out ....

When Smith first came to the door, I recognized old Osawatomie Brown, who had given us so much trouble in Kansas. No one present but myself could have performed that service. I got his bowie-knife from his person and have it yet.

The same day, about eleven or twelve o'clock, Colonel Lee requested me, as Lieutenant Greene had charge of the prisoners and was officer of the guard, to take a few marines and go over to old Brown's house, four and a half miles distant, in Maryland, and see what was there. I did so, and discovered the magazine of pikes, blankets, clothing, and utensils of every sort. I could only carry off the pikes, as I had but one wagon. The next day I was occupied in delivering the various orders of Colonel Lee, and in other duties devolving on an aid-de-camp. The night after, Colonel Lee, Greene, and myself, with thirty marines, marched six miles and back on a false alarm among the inhabitants of a district called Pleasant Valley.

The prisoners having been turned over to the United States Marshal, Colonel Lee and the marines were ordered back to Washington. I went with him, and this terminated my connection with the Harpers Ferry affair.

(U.S. Marines in Dress Uniform with 69 cal. muskets – 1859) - USMC HD

"The Capture of John Brown"

By [1ˢᵗ Lt.] Israel Greene, [USMC]

This account originally appeared in the *North American Review*, December 1885: [This account was written 26 years after the incident and has some inconsistencies.]

At noon of Monday, October 18, 1859, Chief Clerk Walsh, of the Navy Department, drove rapidly into the Washington Navy-yard, and, meeting me, asked me how many marines we had stationed at the barracks available for immediate duty. I happened to be the senior officer present and in command that day. I instantly replied to Mr. Walsh that we had ninety men available, and then asked him what the trouble was. He told me that Ossawatomie Brown, of Kansas, with a number of men, had taken the arsenal at Harpers Ferry, and was then besieged there by the Virginia State troops. Mr. Walsh returned speedily to the Navy Department building, and, in the course of an hour, orders came to me from Secretary Toucey to proceed at once to Harpers Ferry and report to the senior officer; and, if there should be no such officer at the Ferry, to take charge and protect the government property. With a detachment of ninety marines, I started for Harpers Ferry that afternoon on the 3:30 train, taking with me two howitzers. It was a beautiful, clear autumn day, and the men, exhilarated by the excitement of the occasion, which came after a long, dull season of confinement in the barracks, enjoyed the trip exceedingly.

At Frederick Junction I received a dispatch from Colonel Robert E. Lee, who turned out to be the army officer to whom I was to report. He directed me to proceed to Sandy Hook, a small place about a mile this side of the Ferry, and there await his arrival. At ten o'clock in the evening he came up on a special train from Washington. His first order was to form the marines out of the car, and march from the bridge to Harpers Ferry. This we did, entering the enclosure of the arsenal grounds through a back gate. At eleven o'clock Colonel Lee ordered the volunteers to march out of the grounds, and gave the control inside to the marines, with instructions to see that none of the insurgents escaped during the night. There had been hard fighting all the preceding day, and Brown and his men kept quiet during the night. At half-past six in the morning Colonel Lee gave me orders to select a detail of twelve men for a storming party and place them near the engine-house in which Brown and his men had intrenched themselves. I selected twelve of my best men, and a second twelve to be employed as a reserve. The engine-house was a strong stone [actually brick] building, which is still in a good state of preservation at the Ferry, in spite of the three days' fighting in the building by Brown and his men, and the ravages of the recent war between the States. The building was . . . perhaps thirty feet by thirty-five. In the front were two large double doors, between which was a stone abutment. Within were two old-fashioned, heavy fire-engines, with a hose-cart and reel standing between them, and just back of the abutment between the doors. They were double-battened doors, very strongly made, with heavy wrought-iron nails.

Lieutenant J.E.B. Stewart [Stuart], afterwards famous as a cavalry commander on the side of the South, accompanied Colonel Lee as a volunteer aid. He was ordered to go with a part of the troops to the front of the engine-house and demand the surrender of the insurgent party. Colonel Lee directed him to offer protection to Brown and his men, but to receive no counterproposition from Brown in regard to the surrender. On the way to the engine-house, Stewart and myself agreed upon a signal for attack in the event that Brown should refuse to surrender. It was simply that Lieutenant Stewart would wave his hat, which was then, I believe, one very similar to the famous chapeau which he wore throughout the war. I had my storming party ranged alongside of the engine-house, and a number of men were provided with sledgehammers with which to batter in the doors. I stood in front of the abutment between the doors. Stewart hailed Brown and called for his surrender, but Brown at once began to make a proposition that he and his men should be allowed to come out of the engine-house and be given

the length of the bridge start, so that they might escape.
Suddenly Lieutenant Stewart waved his hat, and I gave
the order to my men to batter in the door. Those inside
fired rapidly at the point where the blows were given upon
the door Very little impression was made with the
hammers, as the doors were tied on the inside with ropes
and braced by the hand-brakes of the fire- engines, and in
a few minutes I gave the order to desist. Just then my eye
caught sight of a ladder, lying a few feet from the engine-
house, in the yard, and I ordered my men to catch it up
and use it as a battering-ram. The reserve of twelve men
I employed as a supporting column for the assaulting
party. The men took hold bravely and made a tremendous
assault upon the door. The second blow broke it in. This
entrance was a ragged hole low down in the right-hand
door, the door being splintered and cracked some
distance upward. I instantly stepped from my position in
front of the stone abutment, and entered the opening made
by the ladder. At the time I did not stop to think of it, but
upon reflection I should say that Brown had just emptied
his carbine at the point broken by the ladder, and so I
passed in safely. Getting to my feet, I ran to the right of
the engine which stood behind the door, passed quickly to
the rear of the house, and came up between the two
engines. The first person I saw was Colonel Lewis
Washington, who was standing near the hose-cart, at the
front of the engine-house. On one knee, a few feet to the
left, knelt a man with a carbine in his hand, just pulling
the lever to reload.

"Hello, Greene," said Colonel Washington, and he
reached out his hand to me. I grasped it with my left hand,
having my saber uplifted in my right, and he said, pointing
to the kneeling figure, "This is Ossawatomie."

As he said this, Brown turned his head to see who it was
to whom Colonel Washington was speaking. Quicker than
thought I brought my saber down with all my strength

upon his head. He was moving as the blow fell, and I suppose I did not strike him where I intended, for he received a deep saber cut in the back of the neck. He fell senseless on his side, then rolled over on his back. He had in his hand a short Sharpe's cavalry carbine. I think he had just fired as I reached Colonel Washington, for the marine who followed me into the aperture made by the ladder received a bullet in the abdomen, from which he died in a few minutes. The shot might have been fired by someone else in the insurgent party, but I think it was from Brown. Instinctively as Brown fell, I gave him a saber thrust in the left breast. The sword I carried was a light uniform weapon, and, either not having a point or striking something hard in Brown's accouterments, did not penetrate. The blade bent double.

By that time three or four of my men were inside. They came rushing in like tigers, as a storming assault is not a play-day sport. They bayoneted one man skulking under the engine, and pinned another fellow up against the rear wall, both being instantly killed. I ordered the men to spill no more blood. The other insurgents were at once taken under arrest, and the contest ended. The whole fight had not lasted over three minutes. My only thought was to capture, or, if necessary, kill, the insurgents, and take possession of the engine-house. I saw very little of the situation within until the fight was over. Then I observed that the engine-house was thick with smoke, and it was with difficulty that a person could be seen across the room. In the rear, behind the left-hand engine, were huddled the prisoners whom Brown had captured and held as hostages for the safety of himself and his men. Colonel Washington was one of these.

All during the fight, as I understood afterward, he kept to the front of the engine-house. When I met him, he was as cool as he would have been on his own veranda entertaining guests. He was naturally a very brave man. I remember that he would not come out of the engine-house, begrimed and soiled as he was from his long imprisonment, until he had put a pair of kid gloves upon his hands. The other prisoners were the sorriest lot of people I ever saw. They had been without food for over sixty hours, in constant dread of being shot, and were huddled up in the corner where lay the body of Brown's son and one or two others of the insurgents who had been killed. Some of them have endeavored to give an account of the storming of the engine-house and the capture of Brown, but none of the reports have been free from a great many misstatements, and I suppose that Colonel Washington and myself were the only persons really able to say what was done. Other stories have been printed by people on the outside, describing the fight within. What they say must be taken with a great deal of allowance, for they could not have been witnesses of what occurred within the engine-house. One recent account describes me as jumping over the right-hand engine more like a wild beast than a soldier. Of course, nothing of the kind happened. The report made by Colonel Lee at the time, which is now on file in the War department, gives a more succinct and detailed account than any I have seen.

I can see Colonel Lee now, as he stood on a slight elevation about forty feet from the engine-house, during the assault. He was in civilian dress and looked then very little as he did during the war. He wore no beard, except a dark mustache, and his hair was slightly gray. He had no arms upon his person and treated the affair as one of no very great consequence, which would be speedily settled by the marines. A part of the scene, giving color and life to the picture, was the bright blue uniform of the marines. They wore blue trousers then, as they do now, and a dark- blue frockcoat. Their belts were white, and they wore French fatigue caps. I do not remember the names of the twelve men in the storming party, nor can I tell what became of them in later life. We had no use for the howitzers, and, in fact, they were not taken from the car.

Immediately after the fight, Brown was carried out of the engine-house, and recovered consciousness while lying on the ground in front. A detail of men carried him up to the paymaster's office, where he was attended to and his wants supplied. On the following day, Wednesday, with an escort, I removed him to Charleston [Charles Town], and turned him over to the civil authorities. No handcuffs were placed upon him, and he supported himself with a self-reliance and independence which were characteristic of the man He had recovered a great deal from the effects of the blow from my saber, the injury of which was principally the shock, as he only received a flesh wound. I had little conversation with him and spent very little time with him.

I have often been asked to describe Brown's appearance at the instant he lifted his head to see who was talking with Colonel Washington. It would be impossible for me to do so. The whole scene passed so rapidly that it hardly made a distinct impression upon my mind. I can only recall the fleeting picture of an old man kneeling with a carbine in his hand, with a long gray beard falling away from his face, looking quickly and keenly toward the danger that he was aware had come upon him. He was not a large man, being perhaps five feet ten inches when he straightened up in full. His dress, even, I do not remember distinctly. I should say that he had his trousers tucked in his boots, and that he wore clothes of gray — probably no more than trousers and shirt. I think he had no hat upon his head.

None of the prisoners were hurt. They were badly frightened and somewhat starved. I received no wounds except a slight scratch on one hand as I was getting through the hole in the door. Colonel Lee and the people on the outside thought I was wounded. Brown had, at the time, only five or six fighting men, and I think he himself was the only one who showed fight after I entered the engine-house. There were no provisions in the building, and it would have been only a question of time when Brown would have had to surrender. Colonel Washington was the only person inside the house that I knew.

I have been asked what became of Brown's carbine. That I do not know. My sword was left in Washington, among people with whom I lived, and I lost trace of it. A few years ago, after having come out of the war and gone west to Dakota, where I now live, I received a letter from a gentleman in Washington, saying that he knew where the sword was, and that it was still bent double, as it was left by the thrust upon Brown's breast. He said that it was now a relic of great historic value and asked me to assent to the selling of it upon the condition that I should receive a portion of the price of the weapon. To me the matter had very little interest, and I replied indifferently. Since then I have heard nothing of the matter. I presume the saber could be found somewhere in Washington.

Colonel Robert E. Lee's
After-Action Report from Harpers Ferry

October 19, 1859

Colonel Lee to the Adjutant General

Headquarters Harpers Ferry

COLONEL: I have the honor to report, for the information of the Secretary of War, that on arriving here on the night of the 17th instant, in obedience to Special Orders No. 194 of that date from your office, I learn that a party of insurgents, about 11 p. m. on the 16th, had seized the watchmen stationed at the armory, arsenal, rifle factory, and bridge across the Potomac, and taken possession of those points. They then dispatched six men, under one of their party, called Captain Aaron C. Stevens, to arrest the principal citizens in the neighborhood and incite the negroes to join in the insurrection. The party took Colonel L. W. Washington from his bed about 1-~ a. m. on the 17th, and brought him, with four of his servants, to this place. Mr. J. H. Allstadt and six of his servants were in the same manner seized about 3 a. m., and arms placed in the hands of the Negroes. Upon their return here, John E. Cook, one of the party sent to Mr. Washington's, was dispatched to Maryland, with Mr. Washington's wagon, two of his servants, and three of Mr. Allstadt's, for arms and ammunition, &c. As day advanced, and the citizens of Harpers Ferry commenced their usual avocations, they were separately captured, to the number of forty, as well as I could learn, and confined in one room of the fire engine house of the armory, which seems early to have been selected as a point of defense. About 11 a. m. the volunteer companies from Virginia began to arrive, and the Jefferson Guards and volunteers from Charlestown, under Captain J. W. Rowen, I understood, were first on the ground. The Hamtramck Guards, Captain V. M. Butler; the Shepherdstown troop, Captain Jacob Rienahart; and Captain Alburtis's company from Martinsburg arrived in the afternoon. These companies, under the direction of Colonels R. W. Baylor and John T. Gibson, forced the insurgents to abandon their positions at the bridge and in the village, and to withdraw within the armory enclosure, where they fortified themselves in the fire-engine house, and carried ten of their prisoners for the purpose of insuring their safety and facilitating their escape, whom they termed hostages, and whose names are Colonel L. W. Washington, of Jefferson county, Virginia; Mr. J. H. Allstadt, of Jefferson county, Virginia; Mr. Israel Russell, justice of the peace, Harpers Ferry; Mr. John Donahue, clerk of Baltimore and Ohio railroad; Mr. Terence Byrne, of Maryland; Mr. George D. Shope, of Frederick, Maryland; Mr. Benjamin Mills, master armorer, Harpers Ferry arsenal; Mr. A. M. Ball, master machinist, Harpers Ferry arsenal; Mr. J. E. P. Dangerfield, paymaster's clerk, Harpers Ferry arsenal; Mr. J. Burd, armorer, Harpers Ferry arsenal. After sunset more troops arrived. Captain B. B. Washington's company from Winchester and three companies from Fredericktown, Maryland, under Colonel Shriver. Later in the evening the

*companies from Baltimore, under General Charles C. Edgerton, second
light brigade, and a detachment of marines, commanded by Lieutenant J.
Greene accompanied by Major Russell, of that corps, reached Sandy
Hook, about one and a half mile east of Harpers Ferry. At this point I came
up with these last-named troops, and leaving General Edgerton and his
command on the Maryland side of the river for the night, caused the
marines to proceed to Harpers Ferry, and placed them within the armory
grounds to prevent the possibility of the escape of the insurgents. Having
taken measures to halt, in Baltimore, the artillery companies ordered from
Fort Monroe, I made preparations to attack the insurgents at daylight. But
for the fear of sacrificing the lives of some of the gentlemen held by them
as prisoners in a midnight assault, I should have ordered the attack at
once.*

*Their safety was the subject of painful consideration, and to prevent, if
possible, jeopardizing their lives; I determined to summon the insurgents
to surrender. As soon after daylight as the arrangements were made
Lieutenant J. E. B. Stewart, 1ˢᵗ cavalry, who had accompanied me from
Washington as staff officer, was dispatched, under a flag, with a written
summons, (a copy of which is hereto annexed, marked A.) Knowing the
character of the leader of the insurgents, I did not expect it would be
accepted. I had therefore directed that the volunteer troops, under their
respective commanders, should be paraded on the lines assigned them
outside the armory, and had prepared a storming party of twelve marines,
under their commander, Lieutenant Greene, and had placed them close to
the engine-house, and secure from its fire. Three marines were furnished
with sledgehammers to break in the doors, and the men were instructed
how to distinguish our citizens from the insurgents; to attack with the
bayonet, and not to injure the blacks detained in custody unless they
resisted. Lieutenant Stewart was also directed not to receive from the
insurgents any counter propositions. If they accepted the terms offered,
they must immediately deliver up their arms and release their prisoners.
If they did not, he must, on leaving the engine-house, give me the signal.
My object was, with a view of saving our citizens, to have as short an
interval as possible between the summons and attack. The summons, as I
had anticipated, was rejected. At the concerted signal, the storming party*

moved quickly to the door and commenced the attack. The fire-engines within the house had been placed by the besieged close to the doors. The doors were fastened by ropes, the spring of which prevented their being broken by the blows of the hammers. The men were therefore ordered to drop the hammers, and, with a portion of the reserve, to use as a battering-ram a heavy ladder, with which they dashed in a part of the door and gave admittance to the storming party. The fire of the in-surgents up to this time had been harmless. At the threshold one Marine fell mortally wounded. The rest, led by Lieutenant Greene and Major Russell, quickly ended the contest. The insurgents that re-sisted were bayoneted. Their leader, John Brown, was cut down by the sword of Lieutenant Greene, and our citizens were protected by both officers and men. The whole was over in a few minutes.

After our citizens were liberated and the wounded cared for, Lieutenant Colonel S. S. Mills, of the 53d Maryland regiment, with the Baltimore Independent Greys, Lieutenant B. F. Simpson commanding, was sent on the Maryland side of the river to search for John E. Cook, and to bring in the arms, &c., belonging to the insurgent party, which were said to be deposited in a school-house two and a half miles distant. Subsequently, Lieutenant J. E. B. Stewart, with a party of marines, was dispatched to the Kennedy farm, situated in Maryland, about four and a half miles from Harpers Ferry, which had been rented by John Brown, and used as the depot for his men and munitions. Colonel Mills saw nothing of Cook, but found the boxes of arms, (Sharp's carbines and belt revolvers,) and recovered Mr. Washington's wagon and horses. Lieutenant Stewart found also at the Kennedy farm a number of sword pikes, blankets, shoes, tents, and all the necessaries for a campaign. These articles have been deposited in the government storehouse at the armory.

From the information derived from the papers found upon the per-sons and among the baggage of the insurgents, and the statement of those now in custody, it appears that the party consisted of nineteen men-fourteen white and five black. That they were headed by John Brown, of some notoriety in Kansas, who in June last located himself in Maryland, at the Kennedy farm, where he has been engaged in preparing to capture the United States works at Harpers Ferry. He avows that his object was the liberation of the slaves of Virginia, and of the whole South; and acknowledges that he has been disappointed in his expectations of aid from the black as well as white population, both in the Southern and Northern States. The blacks, whom he forced from their homes in this neighborhood, as far as I could learn, gave him no voluntary assistance. The servants of Messrs. Washington and Allstadt, retained at the armory, took no part in the conflict, and those carried to Maryland returned to their homes as soon as released. The result proves that the plan was the attempt of a fanatic or mad-man, who could only end in failure; and its temporary success, was owing to the panic and confusion he succeeded in creating by magnify-ing his numbers. I append a list of the insurgents, (marked B.) Cook is the only man known to have escaped. The other survivors of the expedition, viz: John Brown, A. C. Stevens, Edwin Coppic, and Green Shields, (alias S. Emperor,) I have delivered into the hands of the marshal of the western district of Virginia and the sheriff of Jefferson county. They were escorted to Charlestown by a detach-ment of marines, under Lieutenant Greene. About nine o'clock this evening I received a report from Mr. Moore, from Pleasant Valley, Maryland, that a body of men had, about sunset, descended from the mountains, attacked the house of Mr. Gennett, and from the cries of murder and the screams of the women and children, he believed the residents of the valley were being massacred. The alarm and excite-ment in the village of Harpers Ferry was increased by the arrival of families from Sandy Hook, fleeing for safety. The report was, however, so improbable that I could give no credence to it, yet I thought it possible that some atrocity might have been committed, and I started with twenty-five marines, under Lieutenant Greene, accompanied by Lieutenant Stewart, for the scene of the alleged outrage, about four and a half miles distant. I was happy to find it a false alarm. The inhabitants of Pleasant Valley were quiet and unharmed, and Mr. Gennett and his family safe and asleep.

I will now, in obedience to your dispatch of this date, direct the detachment of marines to return to the navy-yard at Washington in the train that passes here at I am to-night, and will myself take advantage of the same train to report to you in person at the War Department. I must also ask to express my thanks to Lieutenant Stewart, Major Russell, and Lieutenant Greene, for the aid they afforded me, and my entire commendation of the conduct of the detachment of marines, who were at all times ready and prompt in the execution of any duty.

The promptness with which the volunteer troops repaired to the scene of disturbance, and the alacrity they displayed to suppress the gross outrage against law and order, I know will elicit your hearty approbation. Equal zeal was shown by the president and officers of the Baltimore and Ohio Railroad Company in their transportation of the troops and in their readiness to furnish the facilities of their well-ordered road.

A list of the killed and wounded, as far as came to my knowledge, is herewith annexed, marked, and I enclose a copy of the "Provisional Constitution and ordinances for the people of the United States," of which there were a large number prepared for issue by the insurgents.

I am, very respectfully, your obedient servant,

R. E. LEE, Colonel Commanding.

Colonel S. COOPER, Adjutant General U. S. Army, Washington City, D.C

Headquarters Harpers Ferry

October 18, 1859.

Colonel Lee, United States army, commanding the troops sent by the President of the United States to suppress the insurrection at this place, demands the surrender of the persons in the armory buildings. If they will peaceably surrender themselves and restore the pillaged property, they shall be kept in safety to await the orders of the President. Colonel Lee represents to them, in all frankness, that it is impossible for them to escape; that the armory is surrounded on all sides by troops; and that if he is compelled to take them by force he cannot answer for their safety.

R.E. Lee

Colonel Commanding United States Troops

Private Luke Quinn:
The Unlikely Celebrity of Harpers Ferry

When Private Luke Quinn arrived in Harpers Ferry, Virginia on October 18, 1859 he likely did not imagine that he would never leave. He certainly could not have imagined that he would be popularized in the small town with a namesake pub, an interesting monument, and an unrestful sleep in St. Peter's Cemetery. Here is a quick look at the lively afterlife of the most unlikely celebrity of John Brown's raid.

Little is known about Private Luke Quinn prior to his untimely death. From his military records we know that he was born in Ireland in 1835 and arrived in the United States with his parents in 1844. He worked as a common laborer until November 1855 when he enlisted in Brooklyn, New York, for a term of four years as a private in the United States Marine Corps. He trained at the Marine Barracks in Washington, DC, until September 1856, when he was assigned to the frigate *USS St. Lawrence*. He served aboard the *St. Lawrence* and the *USS Perry* on expeditions to Brazil and Paraguay and arrived back at the Washington barracks in May 1859.

On October 17, 1859, just as his term of enlistment nearing its end, Quinn was among the 86 Marines dispatched to Harpers Ferry. The Marines arrived at the United States Armory at Harpers Ferry the following morning to find a band of raiders under the command of Captain John Brown of "Bleeding Kansas" fame. Brown and his men had arrived at the Ferry to seize a cache of weapons stored at the arsenal there and to liberate slaves from local slaveholders. Local militia companies, railroad workers and armory employees had cornered the raiders and their civilian hostages inside the armory engine house. After a final, unsuccessful attempt to engage Brown and negotiate a surrender, Colonel Robert E. Lee commanded the Marines to attack the engine house and quell the insurrectionists.

Marines Attacking the Engine House (*Harper's Weekly*)

A group of Marines stormed the engine house, battering the heavy door with sledgehammers. Lieutenant Israel Greene – tasked with leading the assault – espied a nearby ladder and ordered the Marines to use it as a battering ram. After a few blows the lower section of the door collapsed and Greene gained entry into the dark, hazy engine house. Immediately behind Greene entered Private Quinn. As Greene recalled in 1885, "the Marine who followed me into the aperture made by the ladder received a bullet in the abdomen, from which he died in a few minutes." [This statement was written twenty-six years after the incident and may be inconsistent with other accounts of the day. Quinn was wounded prior to the Marines entering. He died 4 hours later.]

Greene could not be certain, but he believed it was John Brown who fired the fatal shot. Hostage John Allstadt likewise believed Brown to have fired the shot that killed Quinn. In testimony during the trial that followed the raid, Allstadt stated, "[Brown] fired at the marines, and my opinion is that he killed that marine." In cross-examination, Allstadt clarified that he could not definitively say it was Brown that fired the fatal shot, and that he [Quinn] "might have been killed by shots fired before the door was broken open."

Private Quinn was one of two Marines injured during the assault on the engine house and was the only Marine fatality. He had less than five weeks left in his term of enlistment. In a letter written just three months after the raid, Father Michael A. Costello, pastor of St. Peter's Catholic Church in Harpers Ferry, recalled:

> In the final attack on the insurgents two of the soldiers were wounded, one of them mortally. As both were Catholics, I was summoned to attend them. As Private Luke Quin[n] fell, pierced through with a ball, his first exclamation was to Major Russel[l], of the United States Marines, who seeing him fall, went up to him. In pitiful accents he cried out 'Oh! Major, I am gone, for the love of God will you send for the priest.' I administered to him the holy rites of the Church; he died that day and was buried with military honours in the Catholic graveyard at this place.

David Hunter Strother likewise recounted seeing the mortally wounded Quinn:

> As I passed the window at the Old Superintendent's House, now used as an office, an acquaintance beckoned me to enter. I did so and found there lying on the floor a marine who was mortally wounded. He was an Irishman named Quinn, a mere boy & his suffering must have been great as his cries and screams made one's flesh creep. A priest knelt beside him and like the friar in Marmion – 'With unavailing cares, exhausted all the churches "prayers" to soothe the dying soldier's agony.'

Quinn's remains were interred in an unmarked grave in St. Peter's Cemetery in Harpers Ferry, where they would remain for 68 years. In 1927 local physician Walter Dittmeyer, resident Loughlin Mater, and Reverend John Curran undertook an effort to locate Quinn's grave and provide a proper marker. The trio also enlisted longtime resident Thomas Boerley, whose father had been killed by one of Brown's men during the raid. They identified the spot that oral tradition held as Quinn's burial location and soon disinterred a partial skeleton, including a skull and fragments of the long bones. Brass buttons, bits of a greenish-blue uniform, and a Catholic emblem gave the group reasonable certainty that they had located Quinn's grave. Pieces of the uniform were acquired by West Virginia historian and John Brown buff Boyd Stutler, who displayed the morbid artifacts at West Virginia University in 1955.

Quinn's 1940 Headstone in St. Peter's Cemetery
(findagrave.com)

In 1931, the Holy Name Society of the Diocese of Richmond passed a resolution to erect a monument on Quinn's grave. It took nearly a decade before the monument was dedicated on May 5, 1940, where it stands to this day. In 2012 a local Marine Corps League detachment rededicated the gravesite and installed a new marker and flagpole after the existing one was damaged by vandals.

Most Recent Quinn Gravestone
(findagrave.com)

But Private Quinn's story does not end there.

In 2009 a pub opened in a ca. 1830s building along Potomac Street in Harpers Ferry with Private Quinn – who had died less than 500 feet away – as its namesake. Private Quinn's Pub was a popular stop for hikers, tourists, and residents until the devastating 2015 fire that swept the Harpers Ferry historic commercial district. The pub was heavily damaged during the fire and never reopened – the restored building today houses Almost Heaven Pub and Grill.

For nearly a century Harper's Ferry has worked – sometimes unconventionally – to keep alive the memory of Private Luke Quinn, an otherwise faceless soldier who was among the first of hundreds of thousands to follow in the years ahead.

**Quinn Monument on Potomac Street
(findagrave.com)**

Jon-Erik M. Gilot holds degrees from Bethany College and Kent State University. He has been involved in the fields of archives and preservation for more than a decade and today works as an archivist in Wheeling, West Virginia.

APPENDIX
Senate Select Committee Report
on the Harpers Ferry Invasion
Testimony of Lewis W. Washington

January 6, 1860.

Lewis W. Washington sworn and examined.

By the Chairman:

Question. Will you please to state your age, and where you reside.
Answer. I am about forty-six years of age. I reside in Jefferson county, Virginia. I am a farmer.

Question. Are you a landholder and slaveowner?
Answer. Yes, sir.

Question. How far is your residence from Harpers Ferry?
Answer. It is about five miles.

Question. Will you state whether you saw an armed party at your house, who they were, what their business was, and what brought them there, on the night of Sunday, the 16th of October last?
Answer. There was a body at my house, five of whom I saw, and the other I did not see. They appeared at my chamber door about half past one o'clock in the morning. My name was called in an under tone, and supposing it to be by some friend who had possibly arrived late, and being familiar with the house, had been admitted in the rear by the servants, I opened the door in my night-shirt and slippers. I was in bed and asleep. As I opened the door there were four armed men with their guns drawn upon me just around me. Three had rifles, and one a large revolver. The man having a revolver held in his left hand a large flambeau, which was burning. The person in command turned out to be Stevens. He asked me my name, and then referred to a man of the name of Cook, who had been at my house before, to know whether I was Colonel Washington. On being told that I was, he said, "You are our prisoner." I looked around, and the only thing that astonished me particularly was the presence of this man Cook, who had been at my house some three or four weeks before that. I met him in the street at Harpers Ferry as I was passing along. He came out

and addressed me by name, and said, "I believe you have a great many interesting relics at your house; could I have permission to see them if I should walk out some day?" I said, "Yes." At that time, I supposed he was an armorer, engaged in the public works at Harpers Ferry, almost all of whom know me, though I do not know them; but I am familiar with the faces of most of them. I had not seen this man before, or I should have recognized him. He came out to my house about four weeks before this attack. While there he was looking at a pistol that General Lafayette had presented to General Washington about the period of the revolution. He asked me if I had ever shot it. I told him I had. He asked, "Does it shoot well?" I told him I had not shot it for six or eight or ten years, that I had merely tried it, and cleaned it, and put it in the cabinet, and, I remarked, it would never be shot again. He was very curious about arms. He finally told me that he belonged to a Kansas hunting party and found it very profitable to hunt buffaloes for their hides. He unbuttoned his coat and showed me two revolvers, and said, he was in the habit of carrying them in his occupation, that he had been attacked with chills and fevers some time ago and was wearing them to accustom his hips to their weight. He asked if I was fond of shooting. I said I formerly was and then he said, "You would possibly like to try these?" We went in front of my house, and under a tree we stuck up a target, and fired some twenty-four shots. He then told me that he had a rifle, a twenty-two shooter, that he would like me to look at, as he saw I had some fondness for firearms. He said to me, "When you come down to the Ferry, if you will call, I should like you to see it and try it." I was at the Ferry, it so happened, ten or fifteen days from that period, and inquired for him. I happened to know his name in this way: he did not introduce himself when he came, but in taking up his large revolver, (the size used in the army,) I found "John E. Cook" engraved on the breech of it on a brass plate, and he said, "I engraved that myself; I borrowed the tools from a silversmith, a bungler, and thinking I could do it better myself, I did it." Then, said I, "I presume that is your name?" and he said, "Yes." When I asked for him at the Ferry, they told me he had left, and I supposed, in all probability, he had gone to Kansas, as he told me he intended to go in a few days. Believing that he had gone to Kansas, I was surprised to find him among the number at my house.

Question. You say that he had before asked permission to go to your house and see certain relics, and that he did go there; did you show him those arms?

Answer. Yes, he saw and handled them.

Question. What did they consist of?

Answer. The sword presented by Frederick the Great to General Washington, which he used as his dress sword, and one of the pistols presented to him by Lafayette.

Question. How did they come into your possession?

Answer. They descended to my father, and from him to me. My grandfather had the first choice of five swords left by the general.

Question. Shortly after midnight of the 16th of October, you were in bed and heard your name called at your chamber door, and opened it, and found an armed party with their arms presented towards you?

Answer. Yes, sir. I looked around at every gun to see if it was cocked and found that they were all cocked.

Question. Who composed that party?

Answer. I only knew Cook's name at the time. I afterwards learned the others. The party consisted of Stevens, Cook, Tidd, Taylor, and the negro man Shields Green. There was a sixth man whom I did not see; but Cook afterwards told me his name was Meriam. He was engaged in hitching up the horses, as I understood.

Question. How did they get in your house?

Answer. They broke in the rear door of the house, and in that way reached the back entry that enters my dining room. They attacked it with the end of a fence rail used as a battering ram.

Question. You did not hear them?

Answer. No, sir; that is about fifty feet from my chamber, with about five feet of walls interposing.

Question. Where is your chamber?

Answer. On the front of the house on the first floor.

Question. Was there any other white person in the house besides yourself?

Answer. No, sir; they asked me directly for my overseer. I told them he was not there; that his family did not reside on my place, and he went to his own house every night.

Question. What did your family consist of?

Answer. My daughter had left the morning before for Baltimore; she had been spending the summer with me. Mr. William Turner and his two daughters were with me the night preceding. I was then alone.

Question. Was your daughter the only member of your family?

Answer. I have two daughters, one of whom has never resided with me, and the other was with me temporarily only, spending a few months in summer. She resides with her grandmother. She is a young lady grown. She had gone off the morning before, Saturday, with Mr. Turner and his daughters to Baltimore. This attack was on Sunday night or Monday morning, at the change of hours. After looking around I observed that each man had two revolvers sticking in his belt in front besides the rifle. I remarked to them, "you are a very bold looking set of fellows, but I should doubt your courage; you have too many arms to take one man." I said to one of them, "I believe with a pop-up gun I could take either of you in your shirt tail." At that time, the fire began falling from the flambeau, and I asked them to come in my room and light my candles, so as to prevent my house from being burnt. After going in, and while dressing myself, I said, "Possibly you will have the courtesy to tell me what this means; it is really a myth to me." Stevens spoke up and said, "We have come here for the purpose of liberating all the slaves of the South, and we are able (or prepared) to do it," or words to that effect. I went on deliberately and dressed myself, and went into the dining room, thinking that possibly there was a better fire there; the fire in my chamber had gone out. I went into the dining room, and when I first got in, Stevens said to me, "You have some fire-arms, have you not?" I replied, "Yes, but all unloaded." He said, "I want them," and Cook made a signal to him that he had seen a very handsome gun in my closet. It was a gun which I had imported from England, and thinking he was a workman in the armory, I showed it to him, to get his opinion. I opened my closet in the dining room, and they took out the guns.

Question. What guns were they?

Answer. A shot gun and a rifle, and an old pistol of Harpers Ferry make of 1806, which was merely kept as a curiosity. They took them. Then Stevens said to me, "Have you a watch, sir?" I replied, "I have." Said he, "Where is it?" I said, "It is on my person." Said he, "I want it, sir." Said I, "You shall not have it." Said he, "Take care, sir." He then asked, "Have you money?" I remarked, "It is very comfortable to have a good deal of it these times; money is rather scarce." Then he made the same remark to me that he did before, "Take care, sir." I then said to him, "I am going to speak very plainly; you told me your purpose was philanthropic, but you did not mention at the same time that it was robbery and rascality. I do not choose to surrender my watch." He yielded the point; did not insist on it. I told him there were four there with arms, and they could take it, but I would not surrender it. Then he said to me, "I presume you have heard of Ossawatomie Brown?" I said, "No, I have not." "Then," said he, "you have paid very little attention to Kansas matters." I remarked to him that I had become so much disgusted with Kansas, and everything connected with it, that whenever I saw a paper with "Kansas" at the head of it I turned it over and did not read it. "Well," said he, "you will see him this morning," speaking apparently with great glorification. After some little time, they announced to me that my carriage was ready at the door.

Question. Did they inquire about plate?

Answer. Yes; they saw in my cabinet a camp-service that belonged to General Arista in the Mexican war; I had taken it out of the case where it belonged and placed it in the cabinet; it is of very rare and beautiful workmanship; Stevens said "I do not know but we shall want that," but afterwards he said he did not know but that it was plated-ware, instead of silver. After some little time, one came and announced that the carriage was at the door. I went out, and found the fellow, Shields Green; they called him "Emperor;" it was the first time I had seen him; he drove the carriage to the door, and as soon as I went out I found my large farm wagon with four horses hitched behind the carriage. I said to the men "These horses" (referring to the carriage horses) "will not drive in that way; they are high-spirited horses; they are on the wrong side;" Tidd, I think, went up and said, "This horse is reined too short." One horse is slightly shorter than the other, and they had got the small harness on the large horse; we got on some little distance when the horses refused to work; by the by, this Emperor, as they termed him, Shields Green, was ordered off the seat when the carriage was about leaving the house, and my house servant, one of my slaves, was put in his place; Cook was on the back seat with me, and Tidd by the side of the driver; the other men were in the wagon behind; I only saw the wagon indistinctly, and did not know who was being placed in it

Question. Did they tell you anything about taking your negroes?
Answer. They said, "We ordered your wagon to take your servants;" and I supposed they were going to take women and all, but it seems they did not want women. I did not know until I got in my field who was in the wagon. When the carriage horses refused to pull, I said "These horses must be shifted;" I got down and put my foot on the wheel, and one of my servants came to help shift the horses, the servant whom they afterwards had in Maryland and who returned; the carriage horses were shifted in the field, and they went very well until they reached some point on the road; in the hurry of putting the harness on, the harness came loose near the top of the hill near Mr. Altstadt's house.

Question. What direction did they take on leaving your house?
Answer. The direction of Harpers Ferry by the usual road that led to the Ferry.

Question. Where was your first stopping place?
Answer. At the house of Mrs. Henderson, widow of Richard Henderson; they stopped the carriage just in front of the house; there were four or five daughters in the house who recently slot [sic] their father, and I remarked to the party in front of me "There is no one here but ladies and it would be an infamous shame to wake them up at this hour of the night." Tidd jumped out, went to the wagon, and made some remark, and they went on; they went on to Allstadt's; I heard them take a fence rail from opposite the house; we stopped on the main road in front of the house; I did not hear any directions given there; a portion of the party was left with me in my carriage; Allstadt's enclosure bordering on the pike has a post and rail fence around it; the road on the opposite side of the pike has one of our Virginia worm fences, and from this fence I heard rails moving; being familiar with the sound, I knew what they were taking; they then went

towards Allstadt's house, and I heard the jar of the rail against the door, and in a few moments there was a shout of murder and general commotion in the house; I thought first it was his servants hallowing murder, but he told me afterwards it was his daughters; finding this commotion going on, they put their heads out of the window and hallooed murder; one of these fellows drew his rifle on them and ordered them to go in and shut the window; I supposed of course what their purpose was; they took a number of negroes from him, I do not know exactly how many, and Allstadt was placed in the wagon with the negroes and taken to Harpers Ferry; they mentioned to him, as he afterwards informed me, that I was in my carriage; we then proceeded on to Harpers Ferry. Up to that time I supposed it was merely a robbing party who possibly had some room at the Ferry; I did not look on the thing as very serious at all until we drove to the armory gate, and the party on the front seat of the carriage said "All's well," and the reply came from the sentinel at the gate "All's well;" then the gates were opened and I was driven in and was received by old Brown; the carriage drove into the armory yard nearly opposite the engine-house.

Question. What did Brown say? How did he know who you were?

Answer. I presume he knew who had been sent for, and he at once assumed who I was.

Question. Did he address you by name?

Answer. He did not at that moment, but as "sir." He said, "You will find a fire in here, sir; it is rather cool this morning." Afterwards he came and said, "I presume you are Mr. Washington." He then remarked to me, "It is too dark to see to write at this time, but when it shall have cleared off a little and become lighter, if you have not pen and ink, I will furnish them to you, and I shall require you to write to some of your friends to send a stout, able-bodied negro; I think after a while, possibly, I shall be enabled to release you, but only on the condition of getting your friends to send in a negro man as a ransom." Then he said, "I shall be very attentive to you, sir, for I may get the worst of it in my first encounter, and if so, your life is worth as much as mine. I shall be very particular to pay attention to you. My particular reason for taking you first was that, as the aid to the governor of Virginia, I knew you would endeavor to perform your duty, and perhaps you would have been a troublesome customer to me; and, apart from that,

I wanted you particularly for the moral effect it would give our cause, having one of your name as a prisoner."

Question. Did he tell you what his purpose was; what "cause" he was in?
Answer. He spoke generally of it. He said, perhaps, "this thing must be put a stop to," or something of that sort. He used general terms.

Question. "This thing," alluding to what?
Answer. Alluding to slavery.

Question. Did you see your negroes after they were brought there?
Answer. Yes, sir.

Question. What was done with them?
Answer. They were brought into the fire. The engine-house and the watch-house are divided by a wall. I should suppose the engine-house to be, perhaps, twenty-two- or twenty-four-feet square. The engine-house being partitioned off, is of course about twenty-two or twenty-four feet, as the other may be, the one way, by about ten the other. The stove was in the small watch-house. The engine-house and watch-house are divided. They are under the same roof -- a wall between them. There is no communication between them through that wall. The servants were all taken into the engine-house, and we into the watch-house, but they came in repeatedly to warm themselves, each negro having a pike in his hand.

Question. How many of your negroes did they take, including your house servants?
Answer. My servants were almost all away, that being Sunday night. They took two of mine, and one, the husband of one of my servants.

Question. Did they take but three negro men of yours, altogether?
Answer. Only three there. One other heard something was wrong and got in the wagon at Allstadt's. I understood that was the point where he overtook them. That man who joined them at Allstadt's did not belong to me, but to Dr. Fuller. He was hired at my house.

Question. Do you know what use was made of your negroes afterwards, by the party at the Ferry?
Answer. In a short time after they first appeared with these pikes in their hands, I saw my house-servant walking about without one. My other servant was taken, with my team, over to Maryland, as I afterwards

understood, to remove the arms from the Kennedy farm to the schoolhouse.

Question. Did any of the servants remain with you in the engine-house or watch-house?
Answer. Yes, sir; my house-servant was in the engine-house with me all the time.

Question. Did they put him to any use at all?
Answer. Not at all. They made a servant of Allstadt's drill some portholes.

Question. How many servants did they bring from Allstadt's?
Answer. I do not know; five or six perhaps.

Question. How many of yours and Allstadt's together were with you in the engine-house?
Answer. There was one of mine and one of Allstadt's that I know, and a servant I have known for some time, one of Mr. Daniel Moore's, who resides near Allstadt. He was arrested on the bridge or in the Ferry. He had a wife there, possibly. I do not recollect exactly the number of Mr. Allstadt's servants there.

Question. Did they put any of the slaves they had captured to any work in the engine-house?
Answer. None, except one servant of Mr. Allstadt, named Phil. Old Brown said to him, "you are a pretty stout looking fellow; can't you knock a hole through there for me?" There were some mason's tools with which he effected it. The holes were loopholes to shoot through.

Question. Did they make more than one loophole?
Answer. Yes, sir; four, I think.

Question. How long were you detained in the engine-house?
Answer. I went in there about twelve o'clock on Monday, noon, and I was in there until Tuesday at seven. I was taken into the watch-house first, but he took us out as hostages about eleven or twelve o'clock on Monday.

Question. What time did you arrive at the watch-house?
Answer. I suppose about half past three, some time before daylight on Monday morning.

Question. After being in there until about midday on Monday, they took you out and carried you into the engine-house. Did they take any others with you?

Answer. Nine others

Question. Did he say for what reason you were taken out and carried to the engine-house?

Answer. He did not specify it at that time, but I understood it very well from the remarks he had made early in the morning. He just came and said, "I want you to walk with me;" and we went from one room to the other.

Question. What was the largest number of persons that he had as prisoners at any time in the watch-house?

Answer. I should say, at a rough estimate, perhaps thirty-odd; between thirty and forty.

Question. Who were they?

Answer. They were principally the armorers, the workmen of the armory, and officers of the armory; for instance, Mr. Kitzmiller, who was acting as superintendent at the time in the absence of Mr. Barbour, Mr. Daingerfield, who was the paymaster's clerk, and Mr. Mills, the master armorer, and several others, operatives, and some who were not. One was the watchman on the bridge, I believe, and one was an old man who rang the bell.

Question. They were all citizens of the Ferry and workmen there?

Answer. Yes, sir.

Question. Were any of those men armed?

Answer. None.

Question. Did you find any of them there when you first went there?

Answer. Yes, sir; perhaps four or five.

Question. Were they brought in in a body or brought in singly?

Answer. Generally, one or two at a time. As they made their appearance they were arrested, as I understood.

Question. Will you state whether you heard any conversation of Brown's during the night in the engine-house, in which he disclosed his purpose in coming there?

Answer. I think two or three different times, possibly, he made remarks to the effect that he came for the purpose of freeing the slaves, and that he meant to carry it out. I heard a remark made by Stevens pretty early. He was talking to a young man and asked him what his view in reference to slavery was, and this young man said, "of course, being born south, my views are with the south on that subject." Stevens asked him if he was a slaveholder. He said he was not. "Well," said Stevens, "you would be the first fellow I would hang, for you defend a cause not to protect your own interest in doing so," and he used an oath at the time.

Question. Did you hear anything from Brown from which you could learn whether he expected assistance, and where it was to come from?

Answer. I do not know that I heard any such expressions. I supposed at that time he was very strong. I supposed from his actions the force was a large one. Someone asked him the number of his force, and he made an evasive **Answer**. Said he, "I cannot exactly say. I have four companies -- one stationed" at such a place, and so on. He used the term "companies."

Question. What points did he designate?

Answer. The arsenal was one, Hall's works was another, and some other point in the yard.

By Mr. Doolittle:

Question. They were companies at or about Harpers Ferry?

Answer. Yes, sir.

By the Chairman:

Question. Can you tell how many of Brown's party you found in the engine-house when you went there?

Answer. Up to a certain period they were in and out until the firing became very severe in the street. There were eight, I think, of his party in the engine-house.

Question. I mean from the time they were beleaguered so that they could not get out?

Answer. Then I think there were eight.

Question. How many of them were negroes?

Answer. One, I think.

Question. Was there not more than one negro?

Answer. Yes, but not with us. There was only one negro of his party in the engine-house. There were several slaves, but only one of his party.

Question. Do you know what his name was?
Answer. Shields Green.

Question. What was his color?
Answer. Black.

Question. Will you state whether that negro, Shields Green, was armed?
Answer. Yes, sir, like the rest, with a rifle and revolver, and a butcher knife in his sheath.

Question. Did he use his arms; did he fire?
Answer. Yes, sir, very rapidly and diligently. [sic] I do not know with what effect.

Question. What was his deportment?
Answer. It was rather impudent in the morning. I saw him order some gentlemen to shut a window, with a rifle raised at them. He said, "Shut that window, damn you; shut it instantly." He did it in a very impudent manner. But when the attack came on, he had thrown off his hat and all his equipment and was endeavoring to represent himself as one of the slaves.

Question. Will you state at what time you were delivered from their custody?
Answer. I suppose it was about half-past seven o'clock on Tuesday morning.

Question. Did Brown give any reasons for keeping you gentlemen confined there?
Answer. Yes. He alluded to the fact that through us he expected to gain his terms. He was very anxious towards the last. He was very solicitous to have some capitulation by which he could gain his terms and was very obstinate in reference to his terms.

Question. Did you hear what his terms were?
Answer. Yes, sir, there were several. One was that he was to be permitted to leave the Ferry and take all his prisoners to a point about half a mile or three-quarters of a mile above the Ferry, on the Maryland side, unmolested; and at this point he promised to release the prisoners.

Question. Was that refused?
Answer. Yes, sir.

Question. Now will you state in what manner you were ultimately rescued?
Answer. By the marines.

Question. How did they do it?
Answer. They broke in the door and entered with a charge. In the excitement of the moment there was a gun or two fired, I believe, in the act of breaking in the door.

Question. A gun or two fired, by whom?
Answer. By both parties.

Question. While you were confined there during Monday, was there much firing from the engine-house?
Answer. A good deal.

Question. Did you know of anybody being killed?
Answer. I did not know at that time. I knew the parties who were killed, but I did not know the fact at the time.

By Mr. Collamer:

Question. Was there firing upon the engine-house also?
Answer. There was firing upon it and from it.

By the Chairman:

Question. Did you see any of the citizens who were killed at the Ferry?
Answer. I think not.

Question. Were you acquainted with George W. Turner?
Answer. Intimately.

Question. Was he killed there?
Answer. He was killed there, I believe. He was killed in the street; not near us.

Question. Were you at his funeral?
Answer. He was merely entombed for a short time and was buried recently at Charlestown. I was at that funeral.

Question. Will you state where he lived?

Answer. He lived at a place called Wheatland, about five miles from Charlestown, and about eight miles or eight miles and a half from my house.

Question. Were you on terms of intimate relations?
Answer. Yes, sir.

Question. What was his character as a citizen and a gentleman?
Answer. Very fine. None better. He was a graduate of West Point, and a distinguished officer of the army.

Question. Was he a man of fortune?
Answer. Yes, sir.

Question. A landholder and slaveholder?
Answer. Yes, sir.

Question. Did you know Mr. Beckham, who was killed?
Answer. Yes, sir; for many years.

Question. What was his character as a citizen?
Answer. Very good indeed. He was an estimable man. He was mayor of the town and had been for many years employed by the Baltimore and Ohio Railroad Company as their agent.

Question. Did you know Boerley, who was killed?
Answer. I knew him slightly. I had known him some years merely to speak to him.

Question. Do you know what his business was?
Answer. I think he kept a small grocery store.

Question. Did you know the negro, Hayward, who was killed?
Answer. Yes, sir.

Question. Did you know whether he was free or slave?
Answer. I understood he was free.

Question. What was his position in life?
Answer. He was the porter of the railroad station and attended to the baggage. He was always remarkably civil.

Question. Was he esteemed and considered a man of respectability in his position?
Answer. Very much so. He was very trustworthy.

Question. Did you get back all your slaves?

Answer. Yes, sir; except the servant that was drowned at Hall's works. The others made their escape from those men who armed them in Maryland, and came down to the river, and were put across by a white woman in a boat and were at home when I got there. They must have gone back on Tuesday night, I imagine. I did not go back until Wednesday evening. I remained at the Ferry with the governor two days.

Question. Did you find your negroes at home when you got back?

Answer. Yes, sir.

Question. Did you get back your wagon and horses?

Answer. After a while. The wagon was used afterwards in bringing over arms to the Ferry. On Thursday one of my horses was running up in the mountain, and I went over and got him, and took the negro boy who showed me where he had hidden my gun that they had given him to arm himself when he escaped. This was a double-barreled shot gun.

Question. You lost none of your negroes?

Answer. No, sir.

Question. But a man whom you had hired from Dr. Fuller was drowned in the canal?

Answer. Yes, sir.

Question. Did it excite any spirit of insubordination amongst your negroes?

Answer. Not the slightest. If anything, they were much more tractable than before.

Question. Had you any reason to believe that there was any alarm amongst them when they were carried off; had you any knowledge of that?

Answer. No; I could not see what transpired when they were taken; it was out of my sight.

By Mr. Collamer:

Question. What became of your carriage and carriage horses?

Answer. They were left in the yard, and I went to Brown and told him that if those horses remained there, some time they would get off and break the carriage all to pieces. The clerk of the hotel happened to be there, and I asked him to have those horses taken to the stable. The carriage was a good deal shot to pieces. The carriage remained in the armory yard; the horses were put in the tavern stable, and, I believe, they were something like myself, they did not get anything to eat or to drink for a good while. I got nothing to eat for forty hours. I ate nothing from Sunday at dinner until Tuesday at 10 o'clock. Brown, on Monday morning, came and invited me to breakfast; he had some breakfast ordered in the yard from the tavern. I went to several of the prisoners and suggested the impropriety of touching it, "for," said I, "you do not know what may be in it; the coffee may be drugged for the purpose of saving a guard over you." I advised them not to take it.

By the Chairman:

Question. I understood you to say that they carried off a pistol and sword belonging to your family relics; did you recover them?

Answer. I recovered the sword; Brown carried that in his hand all day Monday, and when the attacking party came on, he laid it on a fire engine, and after the rescue I got it.

Question. By whom did you say that sword had been given to General Washington?

Answer. By Frederick the Great.

Lewis W. Washington.

CHAPTER 2

"The Marines of 1861"

The American Civil War began on April 12, 1861, when Confederate artillery shelled Fort Sumter in Charleston harbor. Union forces surrendered the next day. On April 15, President Lincoln called for the states to mobilize 75,000 militiamen for three months to put down "combinations … too powerful to be suppressed by the ordinary course of judicial proceeding." In response, Virginia, Tennessee, Arkansas, and North Carolina joined the other seven Southern states that had already formed the Confederacy, whose capital was moved to Richmond. Between 90,000 and 100,000 Northerners answered Lincoln's call, while thousands of Southerners volunteered for the Confederate cause. People on both sides enthusiastically expected a quick victory to resolve years of accumulated, intense political dissension.

Union and Confederate authorities organized the largest armies around their respective capitals, which were only 100 miles apart. Each side also created forces in Virginia's nearby Shenandoah Valley, an important agricultural region. Confederate troops there quickly raided Harpers Ferry and threatened the Baltimore and Ohio Railroad. Troops in Ohio responded by invading western Virginia in June to secure the rail line and support local Unionists – an event that helped lead to the creation West Virginia in 1863. Meanwhile, Northern men continued to pour into Washington, DC. But, because they had volunteered for three month's service, any campaign using them would have to start in July.

President Lincoln appointed Irvin McDowell to command federal forces in the Union's first major campaign, which sought to capture Richmond. Placing the 14,000-18,000 men in the Shenandoah under Robert Patterson, McDowell led a force of 35,000 men to meet the main Confederate field force of about 22,000, commanded by P. G. T. Beauregard, at Manassas,

Virginia. Patterson's force would engage Joseph E. Johnston's small Southern army of 11,000 in the Shenandoah to prevent it from reinforcing Beauregard. McDowell's army began moving on July 16. Within two days, it reached Centreville, Virginia, about five miles from Manassas and two miles from a creek called "Bull Run."

Hearing of McDowell's advance, General Beauregard had Johnston join him. The latter deployed cavalry to screen his army's movements, and his men arrived at Manassas by railroad from July 19-21. Many observers have lauded this as the first operational movement of troops by rail in U.S. military history; moreover, orders for this movement came via telegraph, the first time that technology was employed during active military operations. In terms of the campaign's ultimate outcome, though, Patterson's failure to prevent Johnston's withdrawal proved more significant.

Meanwhile, McDowell prepared his attack. As a distraction, he had a division assault a stone bridge across Bull Run, on the Confederate left flank. McDowell sent his main force to cross farther north, and then advance against the enemy flank and rear. The attacks began early on July 21, 1861, but difficulties delayed the primary assault. By late morning, Union troops had pushed back the defenders and occupied Mathews Hill. Over the course of the day, Beauregard shifted forces from the Confederate right to the left, while Johnston moved up reinforcements from the railhead. Both organized a new defensive position on the Confederate left at Henry Hill. Following a lull in the early afternoon, McDowell renewed the Union attack, trying to capture the hill. Fierce combat raged for over two hours, but the Confederates prevailed after a final counterattack drove off Union forces.

(Ruins of Stone Bridge – Bull Run - 1861)

The First Battle of Manassas is infamous for the rout that immediately followed. Many civilians had come out from Washington to observe what they thought would be a decisive Union victory and an end of the war. As McDowell began to retreat, some troops panicked, and many fled north; civilians and soldiers raced for the safety of the Union capital. But the danger of attack was minimal. Confederate forces were exhausted and disorganized after fighting what was then the largest battle in American history, with about 65,000 total combatants, of whom 3,000 Northerners and 2,000 Southerners became casualties. Larger and grislier battles would follow. For the moment, the Confederacy rejoiced in having defeated the Union's initial attempt to squash the rebellion. Conversely, Northerners began to realize greater efforts were required to preserve the United States.

On October 31, 1860, the United States Marine Corps, which consisted of 63 officers and 1,712 enlisted men, lost twenty officers to the Confederacy. Six officers resigned and fourteen were dismissed when their resignations were rejected. Twelve were citizens of Southern states, five were from border states, and three were from Northern states. Nineteen were company-grade officers – 2nd and 1st Lieutenants and Captains.

The Marine Corps officers who resigned their commissions and joined the Confederate Marine Corps were:

>Major Henry B. Tyler (USMC Adjutant) – Virginia
>Brevet Major George H. Terret – Virginia
>Captain Robert Tansill – Virginia
>Captain Algernon S. Taylor – Virginia
>Captain John D. Simms – Virginia
>1st Lieutenant Israel Greene – Virginia
>1st Lieutenant John K. H. Tatnall - Georgia
>1st Lieutenant Julius E. Meire - Maryland
>1st Lieutenant George P. Turner – Virginia
>1st Lieutenant Thomas S. Wilson – Missouri
>1st Lieutenant Andrew J. Hays - Alabama
>1st Lieutenant Adam N. Baker – Pennsylvania
>2nd Lieutenant George Holmes – Florida
>2nd Lieutenant Calvin L. Sayer – Alabama
>2nd Lieutenant Henry L. Ingraham – South Carolina
>2nd Lieutenant Beckett K. Howell - Mississippi

A singular moment in Marine Corps history that is often overlooked or completely misinterpreted by military historians is the actions of United States Marines at the Battle of 1st Manassas (Bull Run). While much has been written about the generals and the grand strategies of the day, little has been focused on those nameless individuals who made up the ranks, whose courage and actions ultimately determined whether engagements were won or lost.

A number of those young men, green recruits when they entered the killing fields at Manassas, would earn the title of United States Marine. Considered by some historians to be one of the less than shining moments in our Corps' history, a closer examination of the accomplishments of those young Marines, under the circumstances on that day, shows that they were extraordinary.

Although considered a Union defeat, the ethos, courage, discipline, and leadership demonstrated by the Marines at 1st Manassas can be compared with those at Bladensburg, Maryland, during the War of 1812, and at the Chosin Reservoir, in Korea, nearly a century later. Their conduct and actions would reflect the very foundation upon which our Corps is built. What follows is a detailed description of those actions on that day.

The Marine Corps entered the American Civil War hobbled by the loss of many of its officers to the South. Nearly one-third of the Corps' leaders departed for the Confederacy. The rapid expansion of the United States Navy further drained officers, noncommissioned officers, and seasoned enlisted men from new ship's detachments.

During a special session of Congress called by President Abraham Lincoln on July 4, 1861, the opportunity for Marine Corps Commandant John Harris to reap the benefits of an increase in the strength of the Marine Corps was acted upon. The Secretary of the Navy, Gideon Welles, was presented with Harris's reorganization plan. The abstract for the better organization was as follows:

Section One: Be it enacted, etc., that from and after passage of this Act, the United States Marine Corps shall consist of the officers, non-commissioned officers, musicians, and privates, viz:

One Brigadier General,	
Commandant	
Two Colonels	
Two Lieutenant Colonel	*Two Sergeant Majors*
Four Majors	*Two Quartermaster Sergeants*
One Adjutant and Inspector	Two Drum Majors
One Paymaster	*Two Principal Musicians*
One Quartermaster	*240 Sergeants*
Two Assistant Quartermasters	270 Corporals
Thirty Captains	*3,000 Privates*
Forty First Lieutenants	*50 Musicians for the Band*
Thirty Second Lieutenants	90 Drummers
	90 Fifers

Provided that the officers composing the Staff of the Corps shall, after ten years' service as such in they shall hold rank assigned to them by the Act of March 1847, be promoted. The Adjutant and Inspector, the Paymaster,

*and the Quartermaster, respectfully to the rank of Lieutenant Colonel, and
the Assistant Quartermasters, respectively, to the rank of Major.*

This plan brought a substantial number of new recruits into the Corps, but
by then there were hardly any veterans available to train them.
Nonetheless, the Secretary of the Navy, acting upon a request from the
War Department, ordered the formation of a Marine battalion for service
with the Army in the first offensive action against the Confederacy. In a
blatant departure from well-established protocol, Secretary Welles sent
orders to several Marine officers to report to Washington for duty without
going through the Commandant of the Marine Corps. He further assigned
Major John Reynolds to command the battalion. Commandant Harris did
not receive official notification of this assignment from the Navy
Department until 15 July. The battalion's staff follows.

Marine Battalion, July 1861, Order of Battle

Commanding Officer:
Major John George Reynolds, USMC

Staff:
Major Augustus S. Nicholson, Adjutant
Major William S. Slack, Quartermaster
Quartermaster Sergeant Smith Maxwell
3 Musicians
1 Apprentice Music Boy

Company A
Brevet Major Jacob Zeilen, Commanding
Second Lieutenant Frank Munroe
Second Lieutenant John H. Grimes
Company B
Captain James H. Jones, Commanding
Second Lieutenant Robert W. Huntington
Company C
First Lieutenant Alan Ramsay, Commanding
Second Lieutenant Robert E. Hitchcock

Company D
Second Lieutenant William H. Cartter, Commanding
Second Lieutenant William H. Hale
12 Officers
12 Non-commissioned officers
3 Musicians
1 apprentice music boy
324 privates (approx.)
Total Battalion Strength: Approximately 352 United States Marines

Marine Leadership

Colonel John Harris (May 20, 1793 – May 12, 1864) was the sixth Commandant of the Marine Corps. Colonel Harris was born in East Whiteland Township, Chester County, Pennsylvania, to an established local family that produced a number of military officers. His father, William Harris, served in the Pennsylvania militia during the American Revolutionary War and Whiskey Rebellion and was commissioned a brigadier general prior to the outbreak of the War of 1812. John's older brother, Thomas, was a naval surgeon who served as Chief of the Navy Bureau of Medicine and Surgery. His brother, William, married Elizabeth Matilda Patterson, granddaughter of Thomas Leiper, and his brother Stephen married Marianne Smith, granddaughter of Persifor Frazer and first cousin of Persifor Frazer Smith;[1] Stephen's sons Stephen and Joseph both worked for the U.S. Coast Survey before and during the American Civil War.

John Harris was commissioned a second lieutenant in the Marine Corps on 23 April 1814 and promoted to first lieutenant two months later. He joined the Marines of the USS *Guerrier* under the command of Commodore John Rodgers that summer at Charlestown, Maryland, and served with the forces that opposed the British advance on Baltimore. He was ordered to the defense of Washington but then ordered back to Baltimore before reaching Bladensburg. He wrote his brother "I could see plenty of red coats but could not get within musket shot of them." He described the attack on Fort McHenry as "the handsomest sight I ever saw... to see the bombs and rockets flying and the firing from our three forts."

The following year he was placed in command of the Marine contingent aboard the USS *Macedonian*, which sailed with Commodore Stephen Decatur from New York in May 1815 against the Barbary pirates.

Upon his return to the United States, 1st Lt Harris was stationed at Erie, Pennsylvania, and then Boston, Massachusetts. From Boston he was assigned to the USS *Franklin*, in August 1821. On his return from a cruise in the South Pacific in 1824, according to family legend, he introduced the lima bean from Peru to the United States. He was brevetted captain on March 3, 1825.

Subsequent tours at sea were aboard the USS *Java*, the *Delaware* and the *Philadelphia*. Promoted to the regular rank of captain on June 13, 1830, he was next stationed at Norfolk, Virginia. After that he rejoined the *Delaware* until March 1836. Three months later he joined a detachment of Marines at Fort Monroe, Virginia, to campaign with the Army in the Indian Wars.[2] During this period he served with distinction in the Creek campaign in Alabama and in the war with the Seminole Indians in Florida. Colonel Commandant Archibald Henderson, serving in the field during this campaign, stated in a letter to the Secretary of the Navy that "Captain Harris while in Florida had command of Mounted Marines and did good service in that capacity."

Captain Harris was awarded brevet rank of major on January 27, 1837, "for gallantry and good conduct in the war against Florida Indians, particularly in the affair of the Hatchee Lustee." He returned to Washington in March 1837 as the bearer of a treaty which had been made by the commanding general with the Seminole chiefs. Promoted to major on October 6, 1841, he served until the Mexican–American War at Philadelphia, Washington, and Norfolk.

In March 1848, Major Harris was ordered to Mexico to cooperate on shore with the squadron off the Isthmus of Tehauntepec. He sailed from New York with a battalion of Marines, but upon their arrival at Veracruz, the armistice had been concluded. He was then ordered to garrison Alvarado with his battalion.

Major Harris rejoined Headquarters in Washington from Alvarado in late summer of 1848. His next assignments were as Commanding Officer of the Philadelphia and New York Marine Barracks. He was promoted to lieutenant colonel on December 10, 1855, and placed in command at Brooklyn, New York, where he remained until January 7, 1859, on which date he was appointed Colonel Commandant of the Marine Corps. At the age of 66, he was the oldest officer to become Commandant of the Marine Corps. He likewise had seen more service than any officer receiving the appointment, having been a Marine for 45 years before becoming Commandant.

During Harris' term as Commandant shortly before the outbreak of the Civil War, nearly half of his officers resigned to serve the Confederate States and he labored to reconstitute the weakened Corps. During the early days of the Civil War, when contraband traffic began to flow from Maryland, Colonel Harris detailed an entire battalion of Marines to serve as United States Secret Service operators in the troubled area, with the result that the situation was well in hand within a brief period.

Services rendered to the Union by Marines under Harris were varied and many. Few, however, have been recorded as outstanding. This may be attributed to the fact that the Marine Corps of that period was composed of relatively few men in comparison with the strength of the Army or the regular Navy. The relatively minor role of the Navy in the Civil War (memorable almost exclusively for its land battles) may be a factor as well.

Harris died after a brief illness on May 12, 1864, while in office as Commandant of the Marine Corps. He had served as a Marine Corps officer for 50 years. He is buried in Oak Hill Cemetery in the Georgetown area of Washington, D.C.

(Major John G. Reynolds, USMC -1861)

As Marine Major John G. Reynolds marched his battalion over the Potomac Long Bridge on the afternoon of July 16, 1861, he must have wondered what lay ahead for his Marines. A Mexican War veteran, Reynolds had seen Marines serve with distinction in that war 14 years earlier, and now he fully expected his command to do the same. Still, as an officer with 35 years of military service under his belt, Reynolds worried about the green troops under his command. True, they were Marines, but as they headed toward their first fight in a new war, across a small Virginia creek called Bull Run, he had some doubts that could only be answered when the bullets began to fly.

The order to the commandant had been specific: 'You will be pleased to detail from the barracks four companies of eighty men each, the whole under the command of Major Reynolds with the necessary officers, noncommissioned officers and musicians for temporary field service under Brigadier General [Irvin] McDowell. The Marines were to join Union forces moving to oppose the Confederates positioned at Manassas, Va. From regiments of brand-new volunteers to U.S. Army regulars, every available Union soldier was being rushed toward the impending fray, and the Marines were no exception. One part of the Confederate Army had already occupied Manassas, a day's march of 26 miles from Washington, D.C. General P.G.T. Beauregard's Southerners, about 23,000 strong, were astride an important railroad junction and in position to threaten the capital itself. The remainder of the Confederate forces, 15,000 men under General Joseph E. Johnston, were in the vicinity of Harpers Ferry, 70 miles northwest of Manassas.

CHAPTER 3

"Their Backs to the Enemy" -
The Marine Battalion at Bull Run[6]

The early days of July 1861 found Marine Barracks, Washington, a beehive of constant activity. Recruits by the score had joined from the Rendezvous at Philadelphia during June, and 44 more would arrive on July 10, all of them as green as shamrocks in May. So many had arrived that the post stable had been appropriated as a temporary barracks, forcing the officers to make other arrangements for their horses. Lieutenant Robert E. Hitchcock described the scene from his vantage point in a letter to his parents. Responding to their query as to why he did not write more often, Hitchcock wrote:

> I must tell you why I do not and cannot write oftener. 1st, I am acting Adjutant and take my regular duty as officer of the day with the rest of the Corps. 2nd, we have 377 raw recruits and they have to be drilled four hours a day and I have a part of them to drill. We are short of drill sergeants, having only four at the post at present, this you see puts extra duty on to me. 3rd. We have to study Tactics and Military generally and recite to Major Reynolds, who is a graduate of West Point, and very sharp upon every point of a military character and the result is that the recitation is three hours long sometimes.[7] Now take all these duties, then consider that we have to rise at 3;30 AM, and you can easily imagine that by night or when an opportunity is offered for rest that we are glad to take advantage of the opportunity.[8]

He went on to say that he very much enjoyed what he was doing, particularly the authority his new position held. He liked having his orders obeyed.

(2nd Lt. Robert E. Hitchcock, USMC)

Another viewpoint was expressed by one of the recruits over whom
Lieutenant Hitchcock enjoyed exercising command. Private John E. Reily
enlisted at Philadelphia on June 22, 1861. An Irishman by birth and a
laborer by trade, Reily had joined Marine Barracks, Washington, with a
draft of 48 recruits from Philadelphia on June 29. To his parents, the young
recruit wrote:

> I send you these few lines to let you know that I am in
> good health and well satisfied with the life of a Marine. I
> never had work since I was able to work that I like as well
> as this. We only have three hours drill a day. We rise at
> half past 3 o'clock in the Morning and drill one hour and
> a half before breakfast and the same in the evening. I do
> not think I will be here over four months at furthest before
> I be sent on board some ship. They are sending them as
> soon as They are drilled to Philadelphia Brooklyn Boston
> and Portsmouth N.H. as long as we stay about Navy Yards
> we cannot save over Nine Dollars per Month. We have to
> pay 75 cents a month for washing and 20 Cs for to support
> the Naval Asylum and we get out on liberty every four
> days for about five hours. I was on liberty Monday
> afternoon and I went to Col. Smalls Camp and seen a few
> I was acquainted with. If I be here in the beginning of
> October, I will try to send you some money and my
> likeness for we get paid every three months while we are
> here. The first of the month was pay day so that the next

pay day will be on the first of October. I feel better here than I have for the last four years. We have nothing to do but lay about the barracks from six o'clock in the morning unto five o'clock in the evening and then we have to drill for one and half and then go to bunk at nine o'clock. We will be drilled better in one Month here than the Volunteers would be in six Months. We get pretty good living here good wheat flour every Meal fresh beef every other day with soup. Anybody that wants to go to church can go every Sunday to any they want to. We go swim once a week.[9]

All too soon, the life that Reily described as idyllic to his parents came to an end. His boast of Marines being better drilled in one month than volunteer regiments were in six was going to be put to the test.

Lieutenant Alan Ramsay, USMC, was just ending a week's leave in Washington when he heard that a battalion of Marines was going to be ordered to duty with the Army and would be attached to the command of Army Colonel Andrew H. Porter.[10] If the reports were true, he wanted to be a part of the expedition. When he got back to his post, aboard the *USS Richmond* at New York, Ramsay asked the Marine Corps Commandant, Colonel John Harris, for assignment to active service with the battalion.[11] Harris received Ramsay's letter on the thirteenth and immediately replied:

I have received your letter of the 11th instant, asking to be attached to a Battalion of Marines that is about to join the Army to which I reply that I have no knowledge of such a Battalion but if such an order be given, I will command it myself and will be glad to have you with me although I fear your services cannot be dispensed with on the "Richmond."[12]

Soon enough, Harris learned that a battalion of Marines was going to take part in an offensive into Virginia. There are no surviving records of any meetings between Harris and Secretary of the Navy Gideon Welles regarding the Marines serving with the Army. What is known is that on the same day Harris sent his letter to Ramsay, professing ignorance regarding the battalion being formed for duty with the Army, Welles sent Ramsay a telegram ordering him back from New York and directing him to report to the Commandant.[13] It is very likely that after posting his letter to Ramsay, Harris pondered the matter. There were rumblings about a push into Virginia all over Washington. It is probable that Harris went to see Welles, presented Ramsay's letter, and asked if there was any truth to the matter. Welles undoubtedly showed him the previous day's request from the War Department for a battalion of Marines to serve temporarily in the field under Brigadier General Irvin McDowell, the commander of the Union forces to be dispatched.[14] Wrote Secretary of War Simon Cameron, "I have the honor to request that the disposable effective Marines now here may be organized into a battalion, and held in readiness to march on field service."[15]

Given Harris's temperament and the great pride he had in himself and his office, it is likely that he was outraged and humiliated at being kept in the dark while plans for his Corps were being made. He surely demanded explanations as to why he was not consulted in the matter, and why a first lieutenant had precise information on the subject before the Commandant of his Corps did. Welles was similarly proud and equally jealous of his prerogatives. Given that the orders summoning Major John G. Reynolds from Boston and Brevet Major Jacob Zeilen from Philadelphia to duty with the Marine Battalion originated not with the Commandant, but the Secretary of the Navy, a clear departure from established protocol, it is likely that Welles and Harris did not part on the best of terms.[16]

(Secretary of the Navy, Gideon Welles)

Harris's humiliation was complete when he learned that he would not command the Marines in the field, as he had informed Ramsay. The actual orders from the Department of the Commandant to form the Marine Battalion were not issued until July 15. They read:

> You will be pleased to detail from the barracks four companies of eighty men each, the whole under the command of Major Reynolds, with the necessary officers, non-commissioned officers, and musicians, for temporary field service under Brig. General McDowell, to whom Major Reynolds will report. General McDowell will furnish the Battalion with camp equipage, provisions, etc.[17]

Before the orders were made known to the troops, rumor had alerted all at Marine Barracks, Washington, that they were taking the field against the rebels. This news was quickly relayed to those at home. Lieutenant William H. Cartter, by virtue of his being the senior second lieutenant, would be commanding one of the four companies. It was a matter of expediency, there being no other officers readily available for the position. Cartter, nevertheless, was quite pleased with his elevation and wrote his mother, "I am going to leave for the seat of the war (Richmond, Va.) where I expect we will have a fight now. I am well and expect to be a Captain or a Seignior [*sic*] 1st Lieut. ... Now do not fret yourself about me, for all is for the best whatever may happen."[18]

Lieutenant Hitchcock wrote home with a sense of foreboding. Things were not going the way he would have liked, and he did not hesitate to speak his mind.

Marine Barracks
Washington, D.C.
July 14th, 1861

Dear Parents:

> Your letter came to hand yesterday. I was very happy to hear from you at this time in particular. Last night after I

passed down the line to receive the reports of the companies, I was meet by Captain Jones, who said to me, Mr. Hitchcock, "<u>Prepare to take the field on Monday morning</u>." So, tomorrow Morning will see me and five other Lieuts. with 300 Marines (raw recruits in every sense of the term) on our way to Fairfax Court House to take part in a bloody battle, which is to take place, it is thought, about Wednesday. This is unexpected to us, and the Marines are not fit to go into the field, for every man of them have been here over three weeks. We have <u>no camp equipage of any kind,</u> not even tents, and after all this, we are expected to take the <u>brunt</u> of the battle. We are to be commanded by Maj. Reynolds I suppose. We shall do as well as we can under the circumstances: just think of it, 300 raw men in the field! We shall drill all day and work hard. I have been very busy all the days this far but have taken a little time to write you. I have left my things with Lieut. Wm. H. Parker, and my watch also, he has my address and will take good care of my clothes, watch, etc. By writing to him you can find out about my matters. In case anything happens to me, he will send my things to you, and you can do as you like with them. Lieuts. Baker, Burroughs, and Parker will be left here at the Barracks, and any of them would be pleased to give you information in regard to me or my matters. I hope the God of Battles will give me strength and wisdom to act wisely and do my duty well. I am not prepared to die, but I am prepared to serve my Country, and stand by the Stars and Stripes till the last. I am well and in good spirits. May God bless you all, is the wish of your

Affectionate son,
Robt.

My love to all, and best regards to all my friends. I am just informed we leave tomorrow evening. Robt.[19]

Hitchcock was not alone in thinking that the battalion was not ready for field service. Reynolds felt similarly. They were in good company. McDowell knew the entire force he was taking into Virginia was not ready for battle. But the 90-day enlistments of his volunteers were running out.

If he did not meet the rebels now, the entire recruiting process, the training and everything else, would have to be repeated with new organizations. The President knew his fears but assured him that he would meet the enemy on equal terms. Lincoln told him, "You are green, but they are green, also. You are green alike."[20] The public demanded battle; so, did the Congress. And so, McDowell put aside his misgivings and prepared to meet the enemy. On July 15, McDowell sent Harris a list of equipment that he wanted the Marines to carry into the field.

Memo for Col. Harris

The battalion of Marines to be equipped as follows.
Arms.
Accoutrements
Ammunition – (boxes full)
Haversacks (with three days rations)
Canteens + cups
Blanket – in a roll with the ends tied and worn from the right
      Shoulder to the left side; a pair of stockings to be
      Rolled up in the blanket.
No knapsacks – no tents. Two wagons to come over for the
Camp kettles + mess pans, and mess kits.

The battalion to start for the other side in time to pass the long bridge by 3:00 P.M. tomorrow. They will follow up the Columbia Turnpike as far as the New Fort and Toll Gate where they will receive further orders.

McD.[21]

Major Slack found his department unable to fulfill these requirements. Recruits undergoing drill at Marine Barracks, Washington, were not issued haversacks or canteens. Consequently, McDowell's orders placed the Quartermaster's Department in a difficult situation. Slack quickly sent a telegram to Captain Maddox at Philadelphia: "300 watchcoats and 350 haversacks and canteens wanted here for immediate use. If you have not all the number required, send all you have at once and telegraph Barnum (the contractor for haversacks and canteens) to send you immediately all he has on hand and employ extra force in making up the balance. If you can get any coats from barracks, do so."[22]

Maddox replied by telegraph that the haversacks and canteens were on hand. A much-relieved Slack telegraphed back, directing Maddox to send them to Washington by express. They had to be on hand by th following morning, July 16.

The night before the march found young Marine officers musing about what the expedition into Virginia would bring. Those who had been selected to stay behind were grousing about their bad fortune. Those who were designated for company assignments were relieving pre-battle jitters by chatting about how the Union forces were going to give the Confederates what they deserved. There was much good-natured bantering over the morning's march into enemy country. Hitchcock did not join in the fun. Giving his watch and other belongings to Parker along with his father's address just in case he did not return, Hitchcock's sober attitude was conspicuous. Those who were making light of the expedition suffered a rebuke from Hitchcock, who chided them for talking about it in such a trifling manner.[23]

Colonel Harris issued supplementary orders for the expedition on the morning of July 16. Major Nicholson, the Staff Adjutant and Inspector was assigned as Adjutant of the battalion. Major Slack would accompany the battalion as Quartermaster until he was relieved by an assistant quartermaster from the Army. The battalion would leave Marine Barracks, Washington, at 2pm.

Map #1 - Washington D.C. - 1860

Before the battalion left, Colonel Harris had a conversation with Private Joseph Pennypacker, who reported himself sick that morning. The tenor of that exchange was sent to the Navy Department. It lent a little humor to the hours of feverish preparations:

> Private Joseph Pennypacker of this Post is on the sick list and says he is satisfied that soldiering does not agree with him and therefore wishes to obtain his discharge.
>
> I think his wish not to accompany the Battalion today is proof that he lacks the material to make a good soldier and that it would be for the best interests of the service to discharge him on the settlements of his accounts.[24]

Major Reynolds formed the Marine Battalion on the parade ground shortly before the 2pm departure time. His staff consisted of Major Nicholson, Slack, a sergeant major, and Quartermaster Sergeant Smith Maxwell. Company A was commanded by Brevet Major Jacob Zeilen, with 2nd Lieutenants Frank Munroe and John H. Grimes as subalterns. Company B was commanded by Captain James H. Jones with 2nd Lieutenant Robert

W. Huntington. Company C was led by 1st Lieutenant Alan Ramsay, 2nd Lieutenant Robert E. Hitchcock joining him. Company D was commanded by 2nd Lieutenant William H. Cartter. His second officer was 2nd Lieutenant William H. Hale. In terms of combat experience, only Reynolds, Nicholson, Slack, Zeilen, Jones, and Hale had smelled gunpowder in battle.

Twelve noncommissioned officers served in the four companies. Only one, Sergeant Thomas A. Buckley, had battle experience. Three musicians and one apprentice music boy were also assigned to the battalion. There were 324 privates. Some had enlisted as recently as July 8 and had just a week's drill. The majority had enlisted during May and June but could not by any stretch of the imagination be considered properly trained. Only seven privates had been in the Corps prior to the opening guns of Fort Sumter.

At 2pm, commands to form the battalion into marching order rang out across the parade ground. Muskets were smartly hoisted to the left shoulders, and with fifes and drums keeping time, the Marine Battalion marched out of Marine Barracks, Washington.

The march to the Long Bridge was just short of two miles through the streets of Washington. The Marine Battalion made the journey in time to conform with McDowell's orders to be across by 3pm, despite the heavy military traffic heading toward Virginia. Numerous regiments arriving from camps within the District were crossing the bridge, most in reasonable military order. The 27th New York was a notable exception. Coming from Franklin Square, the New Yorkers spared their feet by impressing every vehicle they could lay hands upon. Omnibuses, hackneys, carts, and wagons conveying the 27th gave a carnival atmosphere to the procession.[25]

(Long Bridge, Washington D.C. – 1861)

After marching one mile down the road from the Long Bridge, the Marine Battalion came to Fort Runyon and swung onto the Columbia Turnpike. Another mile brought it to Fort Albany and the Toll Gate. At this point, the Marines halted in obedience to McDowell's orders and waited for instructions that would place them into the line of march. All the regiments that were encamped along the Virginia side of the Potomac from the Aqueduct Bridge and along Arlington Heights were converging on the Toll Gate and being segregated into brigades and divisions. While the Marines waited, Major Reynolds, as he would at every halt along the march, put the battalion through the manual of arms.[26] Reynolds, well aware of the less than adequate training his men had received, was not going to allow any such breaks in the march to pass in idleness.

The Marines were assigned to the First Brigade, led by Colonel Andrew Porter, 2nd Division, Brigadier General David Hunter, commanding.[27] Other organizations attached to the brigade and joining the Marines at Fort Albany were the 8th New York State Militia, commanded by Colonel George Lyons; 14th Brooklyn Chasseurs, commanded by Colonel Alfred M. Woods; 27th New York Volunteers, commanded by Colonel Henry W.

Slocum: US Infantry Battalion of 8 companies, commanded by Major George Sykes, a Battalion of U.S. Marines commanded by Major George Reynolds and a Battalion of US Cavalry with seven companies commanded by Major Innis Palmer; and Battery D, 5th U.S. Artillery, commanded by Captain Charles Griffin..[28] Once the different units were brought together, the First Brigade joined the line of march near the rear of the column. The Marine Battalion wheeled into line behind Captain Griffin's Battery.

The march from Fort Albany to the Little River Turnpike was only about three miles, but frequent delays caused the column to move at a snail's pace. The thousands of feet churning up the road in front of the Marine Battalion raised clouds of choking dust that made breathing difficult at best. The day was hot and humid. Sweat ran down the faces and necks of the Marines, attracting the dust until a mask of mud adorned every marcher. Their perspiration-drenched uniforms hung like iron weights around their bodies. Welts and sores from the constant chaffing where a cross belt, waist belt, or rifle rubbed against the body added further misery, not to mention the countless blisters raised on tender feet. Marching in the rear of the artillery brought a route step not found in any Army manual as the Marines side-stepped and dodged the droppings of a hundred battery horses. And each halt saw Reynolds bringing his men into formation, dressing the lines, and executing the inevitable manual of arms. It was well past midnight when the Marine Battalion fell out to make camp.

Reveille sounded at daybreak on July 17. As men of the 1st Brigade ate their breakfast and tended to their camp chores, more troops marched by. The 5th Division was, after an all-night march, still en route to its arranged position. McDowell's order of movement called for the 2nd Division to be at the Fairfax Court House by 8am.[29] That hour had come and gone and the troops of the 1st Brigade, assigned to take the lead, were still waiting for the Little River Pike to be cleared of men from the 2nd Brigade. Finally, the 2nd Division moved out. As the Marines marched, the miseries of the first day, marginally abated during the night's rest, returned with a vengeance. Fortunately, Fairfax Court House was reached shortly after noon and the day's march was at an end.

The Marine Battalion set up camp at Fairfax and spent the rest of the day drilling while the troops of other regiments investigated the abandoned defensive works in and around the town. Some of the volunteers embarked on a spree of pillage and vandalism, looting and burning private property.[30] That night, when supper was finished and camp duties concluded, the men of the U.S. Infantry Battalion were spectators to the Marines forming up once more and presenting "the novel spectacle of battalion drill by moonlight ... much to the interest and amusement" of the regulars.[31]

That night, about midnight, a false alarm gave confusion to the 2nd Brigade. Volunteers ran in every direction. Some formed a line of battle and fired three volleys at an imagined enemy in the woods. The seasoned regulars, roused by the noise, sat up, made an assessment of the situation, recognized it to be nothing more than case of nerves and went back to sleep.[32] The Marine Battalion, not quite so unflappable, took up their arms, but retreated to their blankets before Major Reynolds seized the opportunity for another drill.

July 18 saw the 2nd Brigade clear its camps after breakfast, march about a mile and wait in the hot sun until 3pm before proceeding to Centreville. On the march, the sound of guns was heard coming from the direction of Blackburn's Ford, making the blood of everyone in the column race with excitement, and, in some cases, fear. Three miles to the south, elements of the 1st Division had made contact with the Confederates and were engaged in a fire fight. The enemy was in strength and prepared to give battle.

The 2nd Division marched down Little River Pike for about two sweltering miles before turning southwest onto the Warrenton Turnpike.[33] Another three miles under the blistering sun brought the brigade to Little Rocky Run, almost two miles from Centreville. McDowell's orders had directed Hunter's Division to go into camp as near to Centreville as water could be had.[34] The troops halted, spread out on both sides of the turnpike, and made camp. They would gratefully remain there for two days while their bodies recovered, and General McDowell and his staff put together a plan to defeat the Confederates.

The Marine Battalion spent two days performing battalion drill and otherwise attempting to perfect its discipline. Even so, the men were glad to have time away from the march, for blisters to heal and for the opportunity to wash away the grime of the road from their bodies. Many took time to write letters home and let loved ones know some of the details of this first adventure of war. Lieutenant Cartter, bored with four days of marching and drilling, wove a tale of derring-do out of whole cloth to impress the folks at home.

Willow Spring Farm, VA
Saturday, 20(July), 1861

Dear Mother,

     This place is 7 miles from Manassas gap. Last night I had a skirmish and lost 4 men killed and wounded 9. We chased about 8 thousand Secessionists troops out of Fairfax. A person feels kind of funny when he hears Bults flying around. When you write to Father let him know that I am well and a Captain, and that I have had a fought. I will try and write from every place of any interest. Give love to Uncle Will, Grand Father & Mother. Your loving son,

W. H. Cartter[35]

Lieutenant Hitchcock, despite the inclusion of a few rumors, wrote a more factual account of the march and what had taken place since leaving Washington.

Camp near Centreville, Virginia
Headquarters, Battalion Marines
Col. Porter's Brigade, Corps Reserve
July 20, 1861

Dear Parents:

We have been in the field nearly a week now and have not had an engagement yet. The enemy has fled before us as we approached their different positions. We expected to have a fight at Fairfax Court House, but as we approached their works, they fled leaving a great quantity of flour, ham, pork spears, shovels, etc. The works at Fairfax were good and they could have held us in check for a while but would have been routed after a while by a flank movement. The confederates made a stand at Bull Run which is between our camp and Centreville and about two miles from us.

A fight took place at Centreville day before yesterday, the result of which we cannot get at, there are so many different reports. We have been at this encampment about 36 hours waiting for Patterson's and McClellan's to come up with their columns in order to make a combined attack upon Manassas Junction where the rebels are collected in great force. We shall bring a force of nearly 129,000 men against them: how the battle will terminate I know not. At Centreville, the forces engaged were the N.Y. 69th and 12th Regiments. The 12th did not stand the fire very well for a while but they came to after a little and went in. They were in a tight spot. They were in an angle in the road which was covered by a masques battery that opened upon them rather unexpectedly. The killed and wounded amt. to 29, six I think were killed. I do not know when we shall advance, we may take up the line of march today, and may not leave for a number of days. We are here without tents or anything of the kind, still we manage to live very well. I am well. This is rather rough life after all, in the field as we are without the usual conveniences of camp. The 23rd Regulars are next to us commanded by Maj. Stiaso, I think.[36] Just as I write, four men of the Regt. (23) are receiving 50 lashes for desertion; rather hard I tell you.[37] I shall write as often as I can, I cannot write more today. I was on guard last night and must get rest so as to be ready for the advance. I hope you are all well at home. Much love to you and the family. Give my regards to all that might inquire after me.

As ever, your aft.

Son. Robt.[38]

General McDowell spent July 20 formulating a plan of attack. The Confederate right appeared too strong to break by direct attack at Blackburn's Ford. The stone bridge over Bull Run on the Warrenton Turnpike was reported to be mined and defended by well-deployed batteries of artillery. His only alternative was to make a flanking march far to the rebel left. Reconnaissance had discovered two spots north of the turnpike that could be forded. The closest was reported to be defended, but the second, some three miles north of the turnpike, was not. A strong column sent by that route would be able to get in the rear of the rebel positions along Bull Run. The defenders of the first ford would be forced to abandon their positions, thus allowing Colonel Samuel Heintzelman's 3rd Division to cross the river at that point, join with Hunter's troops, and drive the enemy from the field. While the 2nd and 3rd Divisions were on the move, Brigadier General Daniel Tyler's 1st Division would demonstrate along Bull Run below the Warrenton Turnpike and hold the Confederate troops in position.[39] Satisfied that his plan was sound, McDowell drew up his orders for the morning of July 21.

General Order No. 22 called for Tyler's Division to advance from its camp at 2:30am take up a position at the stone bridge on the turnpike, and open fire at daybreak. Hunter's Division would take up its march at 2am, turn right after passing Cub Run and head north to the ford above Sudley Springs, cross Bull Run and then turn south, driving the enemy from the ford that Heintzelman's Division was ordered to cross. The two divisions would then force the enemy from its positions on the turnpike, allowing a junction of all Federal forces which would then advance to destroy the railroad connecting Manassas with the western part of Virginia.[40]

The Marine Battalion spent the day preparing for the coming march. Major Reynolds, true to form, put the Marines through battalion drill again and again. Around 4pm, 2nd Lt. Joseph F. Baker arrived in the camp. Baker was not originally assigned to the battalion when it left Washington, which had bitterly disappointed him. Late on Friday, July 19, Colonel Harris asked if he would volunteer to bring a horse to Major Reynolds. Seizing the opportunity as a stroke of good luck, Baker quickly agreed.

The journey took the better part of twenty-four hours. Rear echelon security details held him up at several points, but he finally reached the battalion at Centreville. After delivering the horse to Major Reynolds, Baker went to see his friends in the battalion. His fellow officers were excitedly discussing the coming battle, and chided Baker for being a latecomer. During the course of the good-natured banter, Baker was given a choice of remaining in camp or being assigned to one of the companies. Not wanting to miss the chance to take part in the adventure of his young life, Baker eagerly took a company assignment.[41]

The Marine Battalion, as well as the rest of the 2nd Division, was formed and ready to move at 2am on July 21. Brigadier General Ambrose P. Burnside's brigade took the head of the column but made no progress.[42] The Warrenton Turnpike was jammed with Tyler's Division, who should not have started out on the turnpike until the 2nd Division had passed forward. They were not to leave their camps until 2:30am for that specific reason. But Tyler had put his troops on the march too early, and it took the 2nd Division nearly three hours to reach the point where it turned to the north. The distance should have been covered in less than 30 minutes.

The 2nd Division did not reach the road where it was to make its turn to the north until it was nearly 6am. As the column swung onto that direct road, firing was heard to the south. It was Tyler opening up on defenses at the stone bridge. Despite his tardiness in clearing the road for the 2nd Division, Tyler opened the battle right on time. McDowell's plan called for the 2nd Division to be past Sudley Springs and in position to move against the rebels supposedly holding the ford where the 3rd Division was intended to cross. It was not. It was still seven miles from Sudley Ford when Tyler's guns started the battle. Officers quickened the pace of the column. Sudley Ford should have been reached by 6:30am. It was nearly 9am, however, when the leading elements of the division crossed the ford and wheeled left onto the Sudley-Newmarket Road.

Just south of the ford was Sudley Church, where startled churchgoers gasped in wide-eyed amazement as 3,700 Federal soldiers marched past. Just below the church, the column halted to rest before moving on. The day was already hot and hundreds of men dashed to Bull Run to fill their canteens, attempting to ease their parched throats with water mixed with insects and mud churned up by the passage of the troops.[43] Lieutenant Hitchcock and Captain Jones passed the break discussing arrangements each promised to make for the other in the event that either one was killed. Both made a solemn vow to retrieve the body of the other should he fall in the coming battle.[44]

(The Sudley Church – 1861)

As the 2nd Division rested, 1st Lt. William Averell, one of Colonel Porter's staff officers, saw what he thought was a cloud of dust in the direction they were headed.[45] Taking his telescope, Averell climbed to the top rail of a fence and saw quite plainly a body of troops advancing to block the road to the Union column.[46] As he leaped from the fence to report his sighting to Porter, Averell must have wondered what the rebels were doing there in front of them. Was it chance that the Confederate commander, General P. G. T. Beauregard, decided to strengthen his left?[47] Or, had something else happened to alert the enemy to their march? [48] The news was quickly passed on to Hunter, who immediately ordered the division back onto the road and forward.

The delay caused by Tyler's Division had cost Hunter's troops more than a march in the cool of the night. It had cost them the element of surprise. As a result of the three-hour delay, most of the flank march was done in daylight. At 8:30, Captain Edward Porter Alexander, General Beauregard's signals officer, spotted the reflection of the sun on one of the brass artillery pieces in Hunter's Division.[49]

It was eight miles away from his observation tower at Wilcoxen's Hill, but Alexander's trained eye saw only "the brief flash of reflected sun from the cannon but also the glint of bayonets."[50]

Alexander quickly signaled Colonel Nathan G. Evans, commander of a "demi-brigade" at the stone bridge, the leftmost portion of the Confederate line.[51] Evans had the 4th South Carolina and Wheat's Special Battalion, Louisiana Infantry, some cavalry, and a few field pieces opposite the stone bridge. He had been waiting for the Union forces to do something more than merely exchange harassing fire since the first discharge of Tyler's guns at dawn. Then Alexander's signal was received. "Look out for your left. You are flanked." A cavalry scout rode in almost the same time and reported that Union troops were crossing over the ford at Sudley Springs. Taking two of the guns, the South Carolina regiment, and the Louisiana "Tigers," Evans marched to meet the threat. These were the troops that Averell saw from his perch at Sudley Church. Now that his flank march had been discovered, Hunter would have to give battle and fight, rather than maneuver the Confederate troops from their positions.

Burnside's Brigade was in the vanguard as Hunter's Division emerged from the woods to the east of the Sudley-Newmarket Road at 9:45am. The 2nd Rhode Island was thrown forward to Matthews Hill and into a hail of musketry from Evans's troops on Buck Hill. Hunter was wounded and command of the division passed to Porter. Evans then moved his troops forward to the southern slope of Mathews Hill where they fought off successive attempts by the Rhode Islanders to dislodge them. Soon, General Burnside's entire brigade was in action and hard pressed by Confederate reinforcements arriving on the field under the command of Brigadier General Barnard Bee, PACS, (the volunteers who made up the Provisional Army of the Confederate States.)[52]

While Burnside's Brigade was being roughly handled by the Confederates, the 1st Brigade passed through the woods over an abandoned railroad grade to the west of the road and extended the Union line beyond the Confederate left. Captain Griffin's six-gun West Point Battery was in the lead, followed by the Marine Battalion, 27th New York, 14th Brooklyn, 8th New York State Militia, and a battalion of U.S. Infantry. Captain Griffin's battery unlimbered on the crest of a ridge some six hundred yards from the intersection of the Warrenton Turnpike and the Sudley-Newmarket Road, and opened fire on the rebel artillery. The Marine Battalion took up a position on the far right of the line, backed up by the battalion of U.S. Cavalry.

As the battle intensified, the sound of the firing drifted to the capital, some twenty-five miles distant. The women at Marine Barracks, Washington, comforted each other with assurances that their husbands would return safely. The wife of Captain James Jones was glad she had accepted the invitation of Mrs. Reynolds to share her quarters while their husbands were in the field.[53] Samuel H. Huntington, father of 2nd Lieutenant Robert W. Huntington, spent the entire day in church, praying for the safety of his son. Each time the noise from the southwest grew louder, Huntington's prayers became more fervent.[54]

As the fight progressed, the numerical strength of the Union forces began to tip the battle in their favor. Captain Griffin's battery moved forward about 200 yards to enfilade the rebel line. Captain James B. Ricketts's battery came forward and unlimbered near Griffin.[55] The deadly chorus of rifled cannon shots caused the Confederate line to waver. In desperation, the rebels launched an attack on the Union center, but were beaten back with heavy losses. Sykes's U.S. Infantry Battalion, detached to bolster Burnside's worn-out troops, delivered a sharp attack that forced a crack in the Confederate right. Troops from Heintzelman's 3rd Division entered the battle on the left of the Union lines and pressed the Confederates back toward Buck Hill. After a stubborn defense of nearly two hours' duration, the rebels fled the field, stampeding across the Warrenton Turnpike and beyond the hill atop which stood the house of the Widow Henry. Confederate guns under the command of Captain John Imboden kept up a strong fire, covering the retreat.[56] Soon, however, Imboden's guns were silenced by accurate counterfire, and also compelled to withdraw.[57]

Burnside's brigade took Buck Hill and Porter's troops swept forward to the stone house at the crossroads. A last-ditch charge by the 4th Alabama to blunt the Union advance was blasted apart by the batteries of both Griffin and Ricketts. The day seemed to be won and McDowell, caught up in the excitement of seeing the Confederates being driven from the field of battle, declared it so.

The Marine Battalion emerged from the fight north of the Warrenton Turnpike in reasonably good shape. It had suffered very few casualties compared to the regiments of Burnside's brigade. Three Marines were reported killed by cannon fire when the battalion first debouched from the woods behind Griffin's battery.[58] 1st Lieutenant Joseph Baker was close by one of them when a shell struck the man, tearing off his leg. The burst of the round knocked Baker backwards, covering his uniform with dirt and blood, fortunately for him, none of his own.[59] But there was little time to think of those who went down. Battalion officers, screaming at the top of their voices to be heard over the din of the battle, urged the men to keep up with the guns.

Griffin's Battery raced forward, taking up a position some one thousand yards from the woods. The Marine Battalion lunged after the battery at the double time, followed by the rest of the brigade. Assuming their stations behind the battery, the Marines prepared for battle, casting off their blanket rolls and loading their muskets. Porter took notice of how well they performed on the field in spite of their inexperience. His after-action report mentioned that although they were recruits, "through the constant exertions of their officers [they] had been brought to a fine military appearance."[60]

As the Marines formed in the rear of Griffin's guns, the battle north of the turnpike was reaching a crescendo. The sharp crack of the guns, the smoke, the screaming of the wounded, the explosion of bursting shells, and the rest of the battlefield noise made the hearts of veteran Marines beat faster and heavier. Captain Jones, commanding Company B, determined that this was as good as any place to test the mettle of his solitary subaltern, 2nd Lieutenant Robert W. Huntington. As the brigade began to attract the attention of the rebel gunners across the turnpikes, Jones ordered Huntington to dress the company. Huntington went to the front, gave the command, and then walked down the front rank of Company B, bringing the Marines into proper line. As he returned to his designated position, Jones smiled with approval. He would not have to worry about Lieutenant Huntington doing his duty.[61]

Just before 2pm, Major William F. Barry, McDowell's Chief of Artillery, ordered the batteries of Captains Griffin and Ricketts to maintain the pressure on the retreating enemy by limbering up and advancing to the crest of the hill across the turnpike, some one thousand yards distant.[62] Captain Griffin remonstrated against his guns going forward without proper infantry support. Barry assured him that the 11th New York ("The Fire Zouaves") would be ordered to support the guns.

Griffin, dubious as to the soundness of the order, moved his guns forward with apprehension. After advancing some distance, Griffin halted his battery and looked for the Fire Zouaves. It would be impossible to miss them with their gaudy uniforms, but the artillery captain did not see them. Taking his guns several yards further, Griffin again halted and searched in vain for his infantry support. This time he went back to Barry and demanded to know where the Zouaves were. Barry told him they were just then ready to advance and would follow him to his new position at the double-quick. Griffin was still skeptical. If they were ready now, why had they not gone up the hill first to take a defensive position until the two batteries had gained the hill, unlimbered, and prepared to fire. Then they could fall back to the rear of the guns. Further, Griffin added, as a position to shell the rebels, the hill across the turnpike was less suitable than the one behind the stone house at the crossroads.

Barry was beginning to grow impatient with Griffin's reluctance to do as he was ordered. The Chief of Artillery stated that orders came from General McDowell. The guns were to advance to the hill across the turnpike. The infantry support would follow, not lead, the guns to the hill. Griffin was neither cowed, pacified, nor impressed. He told Barry that the green troops he proposed to send with him would not support him. Barry again gave him assurances that the Zouaves would do their duty. At any rate, the point was moot. General McDowell wanted the guns on top of that hill and that is where they would go. Griffin wheeled his horse and left Barry with a parting and prophetic comment, "I will go. But mark my words, they will not support us."[63]

As Griffin rode back to his waiting battery, he passed Lieutenant Averell, the brigade's assistant adjutant general. In tones that strongly suggested the AAG should do something about it, Griffin told him that his battery was under orders to advance to the crest of the hill across the turnpike but had no infantry support. Averell quickly scanned the area. The 14th

Brooklyn was regrouping after taking a volley from the retreating rebels. The 8th New York Militia, having been stung by the same artillery volley that disorganized the 14th, was broken up and beyond repair. Several regiments from Heintzelman's Division were available; the 5th and 11th Massachusetts, the 1st Minnesota, and the 38th and 69th New York. The Marine Battalion, the designated infantry support to Griffin's Battery, was collecting stragglers and would soon be ready to resume its assigned duty.[64] Averell discussed sending five or six regiments as Griffin's infantry support with several other officers who agreed to form the troops and send them up the hill. Griffin was quickly made aware that additional troops were on the way.[65]

Griffin's and Ricketts's Batteries moved forward, crossed the intersection of the turnpike and the Sudley-Newmarket Road, and began to ascend the hill that had previously been referred to as a nameless eminence across the turnpike. At the crest of the one-hundred-foot rise was the house owned by Judith Henry, an elderly widow who became a casualty of the battle. To the nearby residents, the height was commonly referred to as Henry House Hill, a local custom, changing the name with each subsequent owner. That afternoon's bloody work would make the appellation permanent.

**(Widow Judith Henry's House
before (on page 93) and after the First Battle of 1ˢᵗ Manassas)**

In the wake of Griffin's guns came the Zouaves and the Marines at double time. The battalion trotted across the turnpike, jumped down from the northern embankment of Young's Branch, splashed across the stream and clambered up the other side. The crest of Henry Hill was about 300 yards away, and uphill. Fortunately, the ground was open pasture. Unfortunately, their wet brogans and trousers did not lend themselves to marching at a double time. The guns were unlimbered and firing by the time their infantry support reached them. Captain Griffin had detached two of his guns and sent them under the command of 1ˢᵗ Lieutenant Henry Hasbrouck to a point beyond Ricketts's Battery on the far right of the line. The 11ᵗʰ New York took a position to the rear of the guns, while the Marines moved to the left and up between Hasbrouck and Ricketts. Much fatigued from the run up the hill, the Marines had been ordered to close up and sit on the ground.[66]

Rebel artillery had been employing ricochet fire very effectively. This tactic had driven the troops of the 14ᵗʰ Brooklyn from their position on the hill, forcing them back to the turnpike. Lieutenant Hitchcock was heard to remark, "The cannon balls are flying pretty thick."[67] Lieutenant Baker, a few paces ahead of his comrades, heard the report of a rebel cannon and saw the ricochet of the ball. He threw himself flat on the ground as the ball passed right over him.[68] Lieutenant Hitchcock's comment regarding the artillery duel was his last. The shot that skipped over Baker struck Hitchcock squarely in the face, tearing off his head. As he collapsed, one of his Marine's instinctively reached out to grab him. As he did, a second shell tore off the good Samaritan's arm and severed Hitchcock's lifeless form. The two bodies fell in a bloody heap on the ground.

As the Marines looked with horror upon the grisly scene, a loud and heated exchange was taking place between two artillery officers a few yards away. Captain Griffin had spotted a line of troops coming out of the woods to his front. As they formed their ranks, he was sure they were rebels and ordered Hasbrouck to load canister and fire on them. Major Barry rode up and yelled, "Captain, don't fire there; those are your battery support!" Griffin yelled back, "They are Confederates; as certain as the world, they are Confederates!" Barry insisted, vociferously, "I know they are your battery support!"[69] Griffin grudgingly obeyed Barry's order to desist and pointed the guns away from the oncoming regiment. Moment later, the 33rd Virginia Infantry, only seventy yards away from the battery, lowered their muskets, took aim, and fired a withering volley. In a matter of seconds, the course of the battle was changed. Barry's costly error in judgement ultimately tilted the scales in favor of the Confederates.

Horses and men fell like hay before a newly whetted scythe. Griffin raced to the Fire Zouaves, appealing to them to save the guns. The New Yorkers were not able to respond. Moments before, the 1st Virginia Cavalry, led by Colonel J. E. B. Stuart, a lieutenant trying to sell his patent to the U.S. War Department less than two years before, had struck them on their flank. Although Stuart's troopers did relatively little damage before they retired, the attack left the Zouaves on the verge of panic. When Griffin again called to them from the wreckage of his guns, they stood wide-eyed at the devastation around him. They did not move. But the Virginia infantrymen advanced. Closer and closer they came, firing volley after volley. It was more than the Zouaves could stand. They broke and ran. A few brave men fired at the rebels and were willing to stand and fight, but they were carried away in the stampede down the hill.

The Marines, already unsettled by Lieutenant Hitchcock's death, were plunged deeper into confusion by the carnage wreaked upon Hasbrouck's artillerists. Several raised their muskets to answer the Virginians, but most began to edge back down the slope of Henry Hill. The 33rd Virginia fired in their direction and the battalion began to take casualties. Private Frank Harris, a young Irishman from Pittsburgh, staggered from the ranks and was dead before he hit the ground, his rifle unfired. Private William Barrett, next to Harris in the front ranks of Marines, reported his own brush with death: "We faced them on the left of the battery, and when about fifty yards from it, our men fell like hailstones." Barrett fired three rounds at the advancing rebels before he was put out of action. "I think they intended to fix me when they hit the lock of my musket ... which put me back about three feet. As soon as I came to my ground again two men were shot down on my right and one of my left ... You could hear the balls playing 'Yankee Doodle' around your ears but could not move."[70]

Although Barrett was paralyzed by fear, others, not so afflicted, began to slip out of the line of fire. Officers dashed to the rear of the battalion and shouted commands to stay in ranks and waved their swords to encourage or threaten the fainthearted. It was no use; the panicked flight of the Zouaves from the right of the line burst upon the Marines and was a catalyst no threat could deter. After delivering a sporadic fire, the Marines were swept away by the stampede. Lieutenant Baker, while trying to halt the backward surge, was struck in the mouth by an errant bayonet and knocked unconscious.[71] The race to safety did not abate until the troops reached the crossroads.

The 14th Brooklyn, somewhat tardy in marching to the support of the artillery on Henry Hill, was only partway up the slope when the torrent of fleeing Zouaves, artillery men, and Marines broke upon them. The Brooklyn boys remained steady in their ranks and pushed on. Coming to within forty yards of the rebels, the 14th delivered a volley which momentarily staggered the Confederates, who quickly recovered and returned fire.* Confederate artillery also began firing on the 14th and, caught in a crossfire, it too, had to fall back to the crossroads.

As the 14th was exchanging fire with the rebels at the crest of Henry Hill, the mighty efforts of the Marine officers stemmed the flight of the battalion and rallied it at the crossroads. Nearby, Captain Griffin came upon Barry. With undisguised sarcasm, Griffin asked, "Major, do you think the Zouaves will support us?" Barry, the consequences of his actions weighing heavily upon him, could only say, "I was mistaken." Griffin snapped back, "Do you think *that* was our support?" All Barry could say was, "I was mistaken." And with bitter contempt punctuating every word, Griffin spat, "Yes, you were mistaken all around."[72]

After being driven from the hill, the 14th Brooklyn rallied with the Marines near the crossroads. By that time, the battalion had regained composure enough to join the 14th and try to recover the captured artillery. The Brooklyn regiment took the lead, followed by the Marine Battalion and other regiments. Gaining the crest of the hill near the wreckage of Ricketts's Battery, they brought the enemy under enfilade fire, driving them back across the plateau and into the pine woods beyond. The Union line quickly advanced to within fifty yards of the position held by the Virginia brigade commanded by Brigadier General Thomas J. Jackson. As the swell of the attack neared a thicket of pines, the muskets of the 4th and 27th Virginia Infantry Regiments belched forth a deadly greeting. An instant before the Virginians fired, the 14th dropped to the ground and the Marines took the full effect of the volley.[73] Their line wavered for a moment, but the Marines quickly recovered and pressed forward with the Brooklyn troops, now on their feet, and plunged into the pines.

The fire intensified and the Union troops began to falter. Single men, then squads, and soon whole sections of the attacking line turned and fled. Despite the efforts of their officers to steady them, the Marines were unable to hold their ground. Whatever discipline remained from Major Reynolds's drills along the march to battle lost out to the instinct for self-preservation, and the battalion broke for the rear. Reynolds was quickly in their midst, raining expletives on all within earshot; "language more forcible than pious" recalled the Brooklyn men, but his efforts to hold Marines went in vain.[74] For the second time, they lost all sense of order and ran down the hill to safety, intermingling with the Brooklyn boys and the broken remnants of the second assault force.

As the Confederates took up the pursuit, Surgeon Daniel M. Conrad of the 2nd Virginia Infantry surveyed the bloody aftermath of the fight. "The green pines were filled with the 79th Highlanders and the red-breeched Brooklyn Zouaves, but the only men that were killed and wounded twenty or thirty yards behind and in the rear of our lines were the United States Marines."[75]

The Virginia Regiments of Jackson's Brigade swept forward, driving the Union before them. As they approached the northern end of Henry Hill, Ricketts's battery opened fire. Still they came on, firing as they advanced. Captain Ricketts fell to the ground, desperately wounded. His first officer, 1st Lieutenant Douglas Ramsay, who had a reputation for being the battery's pinnacle of sartorial splendor, had gone into battle dressed in the finest linen and silk stockings, with his mustache waxed to sharp points. Ramsay presented a fine target, but the volleys left him unscathed. As the rebels surged forward, Ramsay ducked behind a limber. He nimbly evaded the attempt of one Virginian to capture him, but as he tried to run away another raised his musket and fired. 1st Lieutenant Ramsay fell dead not far from his gun.[76] Among the officers of the Marine Battalion desperately trying to arrest the flight from Henry Hill, was his brother, 1st Lieutenant Alan Ramsay.

(1st Lt. A. Douglas Ramsay, USA – NMMC)

The second repulse was more than some Marines could stand and they continued their flight beyond the crossroads. The majority of the battalion, however, rallied at the crossroads and pushed up the Sudley-Newmarket Road, where it took cover behind the Henry Hill side of the embankment. Several regiments from the 1st and 3rd Divisions, intermingled in the confusion, were using the embankment for cover, preparatory to a third attempt against Henry Hill.[77] The Marine Battalion and the 14th Brooklyn joined in the advance. It had scarcely begun when reinforcements, the 2nd and 8th South Carolina, of Brigadier General Milledge L. Bonham's Brigade, arrived on the Confederate left and opened fire on the Federal flank. This was more than the Northern troops could bear. They crowded back to the protection of the roadbed and ran down the road. Most of the Marines rallied with a scattering of troops from several disorganized regiments in the pasture on the southwest corner of the crossroads, but the fire was gone out of them. Fear was rising in its place.

During the retreat to the crossroads, Lieutenant Huntington found a discarded musket on the ground and, seeing that it was loaded, vented his frustration by firing at a mounted rebel officer in the distance. He was satisfied to see his target fall. Moments later, a wounded Marine approached him holding his musket in one hand and showing his mangled and missing fingers from a rebel shot on the other. He asked Huntington to load his musket so that he could get off one more shot.[78] Others followed those who had seen enough, ran through the crossroads, past Buck Hill, and joined the growing column of demoralized troops headed up the Sudley-Newmarket Road.

To the right and forward of the area where the Marines and the other regiments were trying to regroup, Colonel Oliver O. Howard's Brigade was trying to get around the left flank of the Confederate line.[79] His first line advanced straight into rebel musketry atop Chinn Ridge. To their left, elements of the 1st Brigade, 1st Division, 1st and 2nd Brigades, Third Division, were still struggling for possession of the guns on Henry Hill. Confederate reinforcements reached both areas of the battlefield at approximately the same time. Colonel Arnold Elzey, having succeeded the wounded Brigadier General Edmund Kirby Smith in command of the 4th Brigade, Army of the Shenandoah, smashed into the right flank of

Howard's Brigade.[80] It folded up and the Union troops fled toward the crossroads where the Marine Battalion and other forces were trying to reorganize. When these troops saw Howard's men coming at them on the fly, they turned for the road. Some Marines paid no attention to their officers, who tried to hold them in position. They bolted toward the crossroads in a race with the rest of the fleeing troops, the safety beyond Sudley Ford paramount in their minds. General Beauregard, seeing the collapse of the Union right, ordered a general advance. Brigades of the Army of the Potomac joined with the Brigades from the Army of the Shenandoah, and advanced across the plateau of Henry Hill, sweeping down the northern slope and driving everything before them.

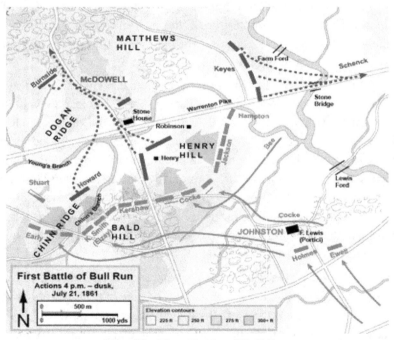

Map #2 - First Battle of Bull Run

As the Marines withdrew down Henry Hill for the last time, Lieutenants Huntington and Grimes asked permission to go back and try to retrieve 2nd Lt. Hitchcock's body. Permission was denied. Overcome with grief and emotion at the thought of leaving their friend's body behind, the two young officers burst into tears.[81] Captain Jones was especially grieved since he could not keep his promise to Hitchcock to deliver his body to his parents.[82]

Lieutenant Baker recovered consciousness around the time of the third retreat from Henry Hill. He was so weak that all he could do was to run down the slope of Henry Hill. Two enlisted Marines saw his condition and gave him support, one on each side. Fortuitously, as the three Marines made their way up Buck Hill, Baker caught a glimpse of his older brother John, an officer of the First Dragoons, riding his mount some distance away. The younger brother hailed the elder and was taken on the horse to safety.[83]

The Sudley-Newmarket Road was the main avenue of retreat for the beaten Union forces. Some ran, but most were too exhausted to do more than keep one leg moving in front of the other. Private William Barrett reported that 200 men of the Marine Battalion were called upon to form a rear guard for a short time before being relieved by the 71st New York State Militia.[84] Then the Marines joined the retreating mass of Union troops. Brevet Major Zeilin had been wounded in the arm during one of the advances on Henry Hill. He walked sluggishly along the road to the ford. Loss of blood and fatigue finally took their toll and Zeilen had to rest. A log at the side of the road offered a crude but welcomed haven. Private Daniel Quinn found Zeilen there. He took the officer by the arm and helped him along the road until a wagon took Zeilen aboard.[85]

Major Reynolds would not be hurried. Averell saw him walking to the rear with his sword in hand. As he passed a tall weed, he lashed at it with his sword, cursing at the same time. Averell felt sure it was the Major's way of dealing with the humiliation he felt at the way his men had behaved.[86]

Some Union troops retreated in good order down the Warrenton Turnpike, but were caught up at the bottleneck before the bridge over Cub Run. Confederate artillery fire found the range of the bridge and quickly turned it into a scrap heap of damaged vehicles. At this point, the retreat turned into a panic-stricken rout. Men fled in all directions looking frantically for a place to cross Cub Run. Wild reports of approaching cavalry fanned the flames of panic. Discipline and order vanished as men pushed, shoved, and swung fists and feet in an attempt to get to the safety of the eastern bank of Cub Run.

In the distance, beckoning the demoralized troops was the haven of
Washington. All would be well again once they reached the familiar
scenes of their camps around the capital. And so they pushed their way
across Cub Run, thinking only of their own advantage and safety.

(Cub Run – Manassas, Virginia)

The Marines were no different than other troops vying for position on this
escape route. Many suppressed their basic human instinct to help the
afflicted and marched on, averting the eyes from the wounded. Private
William Barrett described the retreat in a letter to a Pittsburgh friend:

> At the time of the retreat, we ran over the dead and
> wounded for a mile from the battery and to hear the
> wounded cry out for help have made the heart of stone
> ache. All along the road we had men, only wounded a
> little, who, When the long march came, had to give out
> and lie down and die. For ten miles this side of the field
> they could be seen lying here and there on the roadside.[87]

General Beauregard ordered a pursuit up the Sudley Road, but Confederate
troops became so bogged down gathering up exhausted prisoners of war

that any thought of cutting off the retreating Union forces had to be abandoned.

The Marines lost all semblance of organization during the retreat to, over, and beyond the Sudley Ford. The entire column became nothing more than a mob, scrambling for safety. At some point along the march, Lieutenant Robert Huntington became separated from his company. Totally fatigued and emotionally spent, two enlisted Marines had to help him along the roadway. Edwin S. Barrett, a civilian who accompanied the 5th Massachusetts to the battlefield, chanced upon the trio. The enlisted Marines asked his favor of giving their lieutenant a lift on his horse. Barrett readily assented and helped the exhausted officer up to the back of his saddle.

After a while, Huntington recovered somewhat, and began to speak about the battle. He told Barrett something of his personal history and about the death of Hitchcock, over which he was particularly anguished. They went on until they reached a road leading to Centreville, where they met Captain Jones, Huntington's company commander, and some other officers from the battalion. Huntington got down from the horse, and, with tears in his eyes, he took Barrett's hand and gave him his eternal gratitude.[88]

Above Centreville, the column of fugitives from the Sudley Ford met troops coming up from the blocked Warrenton Turnpike making their way across Cub Run about a thousand yards above the jammed suspension bridge over the turnpike. It was a case of every man for himself. The water at the crossing was deep, in some places over the heads of the shorter men. Non-swimmers would ordinarily have been in distress, but fear is a great source of motivation. As Private Barrett wrote, "If you had seen us swimming across ... you would have thought there was something after us then."[89]

The weary column pressed on to Washington over the roads it had so jauntily trod during the advance just a few days previously. Major Reynolds, having hitched a ride on a supply wagon, had hot coffee prepared and given to all the Marines that passed him. He saw very few. The procession of weary, demoralized troops wound its way through a miserable, rainy night toward Washington. When Reynolds arrived at Long Bridge around daybreak of July 22, he saw a few large contingents of soldiers being held from crossing over the Potomac to Washington by a Provost Guard. Among them were about seventy grimy and exhausted Marines. Pride in his Corps and compassion for his men would not allow the Major to let them stand abjectly in their wet clothes, waiting to be sorted out. Major Reynolds fervent appeals persuaded the Provost commander to allow the Marines to cross the river and return to Marine Barracks, Washington.[90]

The wildest sort of rumors concerning the Marine Battalion swept through Washington. It was reported that all the officers but two had been killed. Samuel H. Huntington's colleagues at the Court of Claims, believing the rumors to be true, called to console their friend over the loss of his son. Huntington was so disturbed by the reports from Manassas that he could not sleep Sunday night and went to the Barracks early Monday morning to learn the truth. He arrived shortly after Major Reynolds brought his Marines in. When he was finally admitted to the barracks, he found his son resting on his bed. Fatherly emotion at seeing his son safe and a sound was "too overpowering to be described."[91]

Major Reynolds presented his after-action report to Commandant Harris on July 24. It was a succinct account of the disaster. Reynolds, in contrast to other field commanders, leveled no blame on other troops for the conduct of his men. He correctly stated they were too inexperienced for the sort of duty they were called upon to perform. It was true that they had failed to hold their position on Henry Hill on three occasions on the afternoon of July 21, but they were game enough to get right back into the fray after each repulse save for the last, when the entire right of the line gave way in precipitate flight. Despite inexperience, Major Reynolds pointed out, the Marine Battalion received high praise from Colonel Porter in his official report of the battle. In Harris's cover letter to the Navy Department, the Commandant, with extreme mortification, wrote of the calamity to the Marine Corps as "the first instance in history where any portion of its members turned their backs to the enemy."[92] He further asked that the Marines be released from service with the Army and restored to their more legitimate duties. The request was made and granted on July 24.[93]

Over the course of the next few days, Marines of the battalion straggled in from the battlefield and reported to Marine Barracks, Washington. Letters were written home to calm the fear of loved ones whose apprehensions had been raised by the alarming accounts in the newspapers. Lieutenant Cartter, who wrote so glowingly of his prospects the day before the battle, albeit with teasingly atrocious spelling, now struck a different pose.

Dear Mother   Washington
                                                        25 July 1861
I returned from Bull Run on the 22nd and was so tired that I could not write before this. There is no use of my telling you about the fight for you have seen an account of it by this time. You received my letters from Spring Hill Farm. That was our last encamping place. We lost one Officer Lieut. Hitchcock and two wounded, and 30 men and got licked awfully. We have got to do better than we did at Bull Run or we will be defeated at all times...

                              Your loving Son
                              W. H. Cartter[94]

In due time, a tally of killed, wounded, and missing was made. The quiet, hardworking, and methodical Robert E. Hitchcock, who had a presentiment of death before he left the barracks on July 16, was killed in action. Private John E. Reily, the young Irishman who thought being a Marine was the best work he ever had in his life, was killed in action. Private John Stanley, another young man from Ireland with the scars of a youthful bout with smallpox on his face, was killed in action. Also reported killed in action were Privates Samuel Clegg, a nineteen-year-old machinist from Philadelphia who enlisted with his father's consent; Francis Harris, a Pittsburgh coachman; Martin Ward, a tall Irishman from Pittsburgh; and Isaac Moore, another Irish immigrant. Privates John Lane and Benjamin F. Perkins were erroneously reported killed but were in fact prisoners of war. Perkins's mother inquired of her son's fate a few days after the battle and received the following letter from the Commandant:

Headquarters, Marine Corps
Washington
July 29th, 1861

My Dear madam.

     I have just received your note inquiring for Benjamin F. Perkins and regret to reply that he was killed in the Battle of Bull's Run on Sunday, the 21st, Inst.

     While I sympathize in your bereavement, it is a consolation to say he died gallantly fighting for his Country and I trust is now in a better world.

Very truly yours,
Jno Harris
Col., Comdt.

To Mrs. Sarah Perkins
c/o Thomas Marshall, Esq.
Sycamore Street
South Camden, New Jersey[95]

A few days later, Mrs. Perkins received the joyous news that her son, previously reported killed in battle was, in actuality, a prisoner of war. He had been wounded during the battle and had fallen into the hands of the rebels and was being held at Richmond.[96]

To another worried relative, Harris wrote,

Miss Mary Barrett:

     I have just rec'd. your letter asking for your brother, John Barrett, who was in the Battle of Bull's Run, on Sunday, the 21st, Inst., and, I regret to say he is one of the fourteen missing. He may be a prisoner, and, in that event, he will get back to his friends. But, in the other event, we have the consolation of knowing he was engaged in his country's cause.[97]

Private George Lewis, a blacksmith who enlisted at Philadelphia on June 17, was initially reported missing. His status was subsequently changed to "supposedly dead" when reports of prisoners taken during the battle failed to list his name.

The list of wounded was headed by Brevet Major Jacob Zeilen, who suffered a gunshot wound to the fleshy part of his left arm. He was back on duty on July 23, however. Also back on duty without missing much time were 2nd Lieutenants John H. Grimes, who suffered a minor wound, and William H. Hale, whose leg was wound was reported to be serious. The wounded enlisted men were Privates Joshua Etchells, with a gunshot wound to his right hand, crushing the ring and middle finger; Edward H. Howell, with a canister wound crushing the left hand; John McGuigan, wounded in the left shoulder while advancing up Henry Hill, and George Bowers, who contracted typhoid fever while hospitalized and died on August 16. Others reported wounded were Privates Allen W. Dodge, Daniel Figer, William Lang, John McKenna, Henry McCann, Michael Wheelan, John Rannahan, Thomas Potter, and John A. Cook (in actuality a prisoner of war).[98]

Reported missing and presumed to be in the hands of the enemy were Privates Henry Clark, a Canadian who came to the United States seeking employment and finding none, enlisted in the Marine Corps; Abel J. Wood, who had family in Massachusetts and New Jersey concerned about his fate; Henry Beans, whose family did not know if he had been killed at Bull Run or taken prisoner, and anguished for months hoping for the later; John Barrett, who was taken as a prisoner when the rebels discovered him hiding in a water-filled ditch after the last repulse of the Federal troops from Henry Hill; William Stewart, who had spent five years on the Great Plains with the Army before enlisting as a Marine; Michael Cannon, whose mother suffered so severe a shock, believing her son had been killed at Bull Run, that she collapsed and was confined to her bed until he was repatriated in June 1862; and Robert Duncanson, who was severely wounded in the leg by a shell fragment while advancing up Henry Hill with the battalion and left behind during the retreat.[99] Others reported missing were Private Frederick Otto, left behind on the battlefield with a gunshot wound to his right leg; Corporal Garrett Steiner, with a gunshot wound to the right shin and left on the battlefield; Privates Jacob Kressler, Edward Foley, William Bradford, John Slemmons, Hugh McCoy, George Hunt, and John Lane (also taken prisoner).

Some of the Bull Run prisoners of war were treated kindly following the battle. Private William Stewart was taken to the General Hospital in Charlottesville, where his wounded leg was treated on the evening of July 21, 1861. Private Henry Clark wrote to his sister from Richmond that "we are well-treated here. We get the same rations as their own soldiers."[100] Others endured a different introduction to life as a prisoner of war. Corporal Garrett Steiner lay on the battlefield for two days with his wounded leg before he was sent to Richmond on a livestock car.[101]

With the exception of those too badly wounded to be mobile, all those captured at Bull Run were sent to Liggon & Company's Tobacco Factory at the corner of Main and 25th Streets in Richmond.[102] The non-commissioned officers and enlisted men were crowded into the second and top floors of the three-story, 30-foot-by-70-foot building. The prison was also known as "Rocketts, No. 1," named for Richmond's waterfront slum district on the James River. Between September 1861 and February 1862, most of the prisoners of war were transferred from Richmond to prisons in New Orleans, Tuscaloosa, Alabama, and Salisbury, North Carolina.* Those who were still incapacitated by their battlefield wounds were paroled and sent by flag of truce boat to the James River for release.[103]

Privates George Hunt, Hugh McCoy, John Lane, Michael Cannon, Henry Clark, Edward Foley, John Cook, Jacob Kressler, and John Slemons were sent to the Old Parish Prison in New Orleans, a disease-ridden, rat-infested, hellhole of filth. The wretched diet made scurvy a common bond of the prisoners. Tuberculosis and other diseases flourished in the close confinement and filthy conditions.[104] After many weeks of abominable detention at Old Parish, they were rescued from the dungeon-like prison by the approach of a Union fleet under Captain David G. Farragut.[105] Fearing a sudden move against the Crescent City, Confederate authorities removed the prisoners on February 6, 1862, and sent them to Salisbury, North Carolina.[106]

The prison at Salisbury was an old cotton factory, a veritable palace by comparison to the black hole of New Orleans. Here the captured Marines were joined by Corporal Garrett Steiner and Private William Bradford, who had been confined at Tuscaloosa since leaving Richmond. All the prisoners were finally paroled at the end of May or early June 1862 and sent through the lines to General Burnside's forces at New Bern, North Carolina.[107] From there they were sent by ship to the Brooklyn Navy Yard, where they reported to Major Addison Garland, commanding Marine Barracks, Brooklyn, between June 2-13, 1862.[108] Garland was appalled at their condition. Their clothing could scarcely be dignified by the term. Their physical health was deplorable. However, new uniforms would make them presentable and a return to the drill field would give them hearty appetites to recover from weight loss. Since they were restricted from resuming active service by the conditions of their paroles, Garland was instructed to keep them on duty within the confines of the barracks.[109]

There were Confederate prisoners of war taken at the battle as well. These unlucky troops were brought back to Washington with the defeated army and kept at the headquarters of Brigadier General Joseph K. F. Mansfield, commander of the Washington District. Later, they were marched to confinement at the Old Capitol Prison on First Street. One group was escorted by a detachment of Marines. As the column reached the Treasury Building, a crowd of soldiers and civilians began taunting the rebels, cursed, and threw mud at them as they passed. Some were not satisfied with these simple insults and began clamoring for sterner action. Tales of atrocities committed upon the Union dead and wounded by the victorious Confederates after the battle ended quickly spread through the gathering. Soon the crowd was screaming for their blood, and pressed forward, shouting, "Kill them! Kill them!" The Marines quickly formed a protective ring around their charges and lowered their bayoneted rifles. The situation nearly got out of hand, but the hard work of the Marines stayed the crowd and the prisoners were safely moved out of danger.

Some bright spots were found in the gloom of the Bull Run defeat. Several Marines had distinguished themselves on the battlefield and were promoted in recognition of their courage. Corporal Smith Maxwell, who had been elevated to quartermaster sergeant when the battalion was formed, advanced to the rank of sergeant on July 23. Privates John Henry Denig and Richard C. Oates were promoted to corporal on July 24. Denig, a printer working at Indianapolis, Indiana, when the war broke out, was recommended for a commission by several prominent Indianapolis citizens in May 1861 but was disappointed in his objective when he learned there were no vacancies. He then enlisted as a private, determined to earn his commission through the ranks.[110] His promotion to the rank of corporal for battlefield service was the first step toward his goal. Denig would be heard from again. Two other Marines who survived the battle, Privates Richard Binder and John Rannahan, would also leave their marks in Marine Corps history.

Equipment of every type was left behind on the battlefield by the Marines during the retreat; muskets, haversacks, bayonet belts, cartridge belts – anything that impeded flight – was cast away. Needless to say, the blankets that were removed from their shoulders and piled on the ground, as they formed behind Griffin's Battery on the morning of July 21, were not retrieved.[111] One all important item was brought safely away from the battlefield as an unknown member of the color party made sure the battle-scarred flag did not fall into the hands of the enemy.[112]

Private   U.S.S. "Macedonian"
Key West, Fla.
July 29, 1861

Dear Colonel.

I have seen by the newspapers that a battalion of Marines is serving with the Army, and I write to ask of you as a geta favor to procure me orders to serve with it. As I have been so long under your command, I hardly think it is necessary to remind you of the qualifications which I hope I possess for this duty. As I am so near promotion, I venture to think that I might be there in a position to render more useful service at a time when our country must need those of every officer, and particularly those who have seen similar duty before. I cannot remain satisfied that so many of my comrades are so serving without advancing my claim upon your notice for a like favor. This ship will remain here at least two weeks more, it is thought, and as steamers are continually arriving from New York, I hope that there will be no difficulty in sending an officer to relieve me.

I have taken great pains to instruct the men under my command in their various duties and they are well instructed in Light Inf. Tactics and the drill for Skirmishers which they have practiced on shore at Vera Cruz. A younger officer than myself will have no trouble in commanding them, and I most earnestly ask that you not refuse me this opportunity of serving my country in a more useful manner than at present and in the position of a true soldier, in the field. I remain dear Colonel,

Very truly,
Your Obdt. Svt.
G. McCawley

Col. John Harris
Comdt. U.S.M.C.
Washn.[113]

It must have pleased Commandant Harris to receive McCawley's request for active field service, even though it was penned and arrived long after the battalion had returned to Washington.

Another belated petition for field duty arrived from New York and likely buoyed Harris's sagging post-Bull Run spirits.

U.S. Steamer Richmond
New York, July 24th, 1861

Sir-

Understanding that a Marine Battalion has gone into the field, we earnestly and respectfully request that we may be allowed to join it. We are on board the Richmond, lately from the Mediterranean, are old soldiers, having been in the field before in the Mexican and Indian Wars and prefer active service. There are a number of recruits in the Barracks who would willingly take our place on board ship and do ship duty equally well. Hoping to receive a favorable answer, we remain

Very Respectfully,
James Stuart
Wm. Firth
Jas. Gurley
And others.
Privates, U. S. M.

Col. J. Harris
Commdg. Marines
Washington.[114]

There were a number of privates at Marine Barracks, Washington, still shaken from their experiences at Bull Run who would have gladly let the "old soldiers" fill their brogans on the afternoon of July 21, 1861.

(Sudley Ford – Manassas, Virginia)

CHAPTER 4

The Battle of 1st Manassas
Staff Ride of the Marine Battalion

The ground you will be traversing during the conduct of this staff ride will be the same ground the Marine Battalion marched across in 1861. In many cases, you will literally be walking in the footsteps of the "Marines of '61'."

A word of safety: The center of the 1st Manassas Battlefield is intersected by two heavily traveled highways, U.S. 29/Warrenton Turnpike and VA 234/Sudley Road. These modern-day roads follow the 1861 road trace and played a major role in the battle. Traffic along these roads can be heavy during the hours of commuter traffic and caution should be used when travelling along these routes.

Stop 1 – Marine Barracks, Washington D.C.

Orientation: Marine Barracks, Washington DC, is located on the corner of 8th and I Streets in Southeast Washington, DC. "8th & I," is the oldest active post in the Marine Corps. The Marine Barracks was founded in 1801 by President Thomas Jefferson and Lieutenant Colonel William Ward Burrows. The 1861 perimeter footprint of the Barracks is still maintained to this day.

**Marine Barracks Washington, main gate,
post 1 at the corner of 8th and I Streets, SE Washington, DC.**

Background: In early July 1861, the Secretary of the Navy, Gideon Wells, acting on a request from the War Department, ordered the formation of a Marine Battalion for service with the Army in the planned upcoming offensive of the war. Secretary Welles sent orders to several Marine officers to report to Washington for duty with the newly formed Marine Battalion. On July 15, Marine Corps Commandant Colonel John Harris received orders stating, "You will be pleased to detail from the barracks four companies … the whole under the command of Major Reynolds … for temporary field duty under [Army] Brigadier General Irvin McDowell … [The Army] will furnish the battalion with camp equipage, provisions, etc."

The Marine Battalion consisted of twelve officers and 336 enlisted men. Of the Marines to be drawn from Marine Barracks Washington, only six officers, nine NCOs, and seven privates had been in the Corps prior to the start of the war, with only a handful having seen any combat service. The Marines were equally ill- prepared regarding equipment. Most of the Marines were recruits with only a few weeks of service and have yet to been issued field equipment. There were insufficient supplies on hand to issue. The Marines were ordered to roll their sleeping blankets, with a spare pair of socks inside, and wear it tied over their shoulder as no knapsacks were available. Requests were submitted to the Philadelphia Supply Depot for canteens, haversacks, and watchcoats. Major Reynolds assigned his Quartermaster Sergeant to "make haste" with retrieving and issuing of canteens and haversacks.

"The United States Marines and Marine Barracks at Washington."
(*Harper's Weekly*, June 1861)

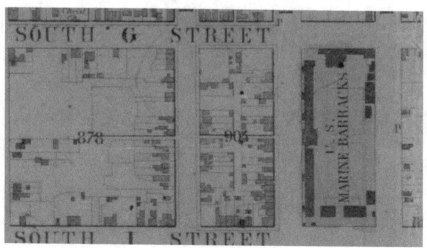

The Marine Barracks as depicted on the 1857 Boschke map of Washington.
(Library of Congress)

**Marine Battalion in front of Home of the Commandant, Marine Barracks,
1864 (Library of Congress)**

**United States Marine Private circa 1861 [portrayed by GySgt. Steve
Sullivan, USMC. (USMCHC)]**

**Reproduction Marine Corps Organizational Colors,
July 1861. (USMCHC)**

Major John G. Reynolds, USMC

Major John G. Reynolds was assigned as the Marine Battalion's commanding officer. He was an experienced 60-year old officer and a hard-bitten veteran of both the Seminole and Mexican Wars. He recognized the shortcomings of his force and used every opportunity to train his men in the manual of arms and drill which would be needed in combat.

Lieutenant Robert Hitchcock, assigned to Company C, of the Marine Battalion noted in a letter to his family dated July 14, 1861, "We shall do as well as we can under the circumstances: just think of it, 300 raw men in the field! We shall drill all day and work hard." Modern-day drill and ceremony are the descendants of those used by nineteenth-century combat formations. The tactical legacy of the eighteenth century had emphasized close-order formations of soldiers trained to maneuver in concert and fire by volleys. These "linear" tactics stressed the tactical offensive. Assault troops advanced in line, two ranks deep, with cadenced steps, stopping to fire volleys on command and finally rushing the last few yards to pierce the enemy line with a bayonet charge. These tactics were adequate for troops armed with single-shot, muzzle-loading, smoothbore muskets with an effective range of about eighty yards. The close-order formation was therefore necessary to concentrate the firepower of these inaccurate weapons. Bayonet charges might then succeed because infantry could rush the last eighty yards before the defending infantrymen could reload their muskets after firing a volley.

Major Reynolds received orders on July 16, 1861, to depart for operations: "You will be pleased to detail from the barracks four companies of eighty men each, the whole under the command of Major Reynolds with the necessary officers, noncommissioned officers and musicians for temporary field service under Brigadier General McDowell."

Background: The Marine Battalion was assigned to the 1st Brigade of the 2nd Army Division and deployed in marching order just behind Battery D, 2nd U.S. Artillery commanded by Captain Charles Griffin. The brigade order of battle was as follows:

1st Brigade, 2nd Division, Col. Andrew Porter

8th New York (Militia): Col. George Lyons

14th New York (Militia): Col. Alfred M. Wood, Lt.Col. Edward B. Fowler

27th New York: Col. Henry W. Slocum, Maj. Joseph J. Bartlett

United States Infantry Battalion (8 companies): Maj. George Sykes

United States Marine Corps Battalion (4 companies): Maj. John G. Reynolds

United States Cavalry Battalion (7 companies): Maj. Innis N. Palmer

5th United States Artillery, Company D: Capt. Charles Griffin

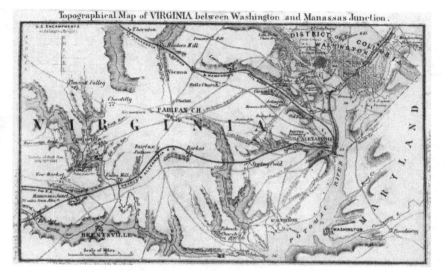

**Topographical map of Virginia between Washington
and Manassas Junction, 1861 (Library of Congress)**

The route of the Marine Battalion, along with Porter's Brigade, began in the vicinity of the Washington Navy Yard, just a few short blocks from the Marine Barracks. Like any modern-day march or parade composed of multiple units, the beginning of the march for Porter's Brigade started in a similar fashion. Lead elements stepped off on the march while trailing elements stood by as minutes turned into an hour as they waited for their turn to join the march. The column eventually stretched for over three miles before all elements had joined in. The Marines fell in near the end of the brigade and marched in column formation to the Potomac River crossing at the Long Bridge.

(Library of Congress)

Colonel David Hunter's Division would make it as far as Annandale on the first day's march before going into camp for the night. It would step off the next morning, July 17, marching down the modern Little River Turnpike with Burnside's brigade in the lead. The column approached Fairfax Courthouse around noon. It was a slow and deliberate march as enemy contact was expected and green troops, though anxious for a scrap, proceeded very cautiously, resulting in the lead elements arriving in Fairfax Courthouse some four hours behind schedule.

> The route we took in going to Manassas Gap was by Arlington Heights and thence by Fairfax Court House, where several batteries had been erected. This was the first time we knew we had to fight; they never told us where we were going till then. When we were about a mile from the place, they got us to load our muskets. We were the first up to the battery, where we were drawn up in line of battle, when we found that the rebels had fled to Manassas. Then the cavalry was sent in hot pursuit of the enemy but failed to overtake them. We camped in Fairfax that night, and the boys enjoyed themselves by burning down the houses of the secessionists. Next morning, we took the march again, and went to Centreville by night; here we encamped two days. – Private William Barrett, U.S. Marine Battalion

All day, during the marches to the west on July 17 and 18, Major Reynolds supervised the training of his battalion. While the volunteer units rested on the roadside, Reynolds's men drilled. Reynolds knew that the key to success for his force of raw recruits would be the steadiness of focused drill while under the fire from the enemy. The Army went into camp near Centreville, Virginia on the evening of July 18. Major Reynolds again looked to the development of his force and continued with the disciplined training plan.

Stop 2 – Centreville, Virginia, Second Division camp two miles Southeast of town near modern day Lee Highway and Centreville Road intersection.

Orientation: Stop 2 is located at the intersection of Machen Road and U.S. Route 29 (Lee Highway), on the grounds of the Centreville Public Library located at the southwest corner of the intersection at 14200 Saint Germain Drive, Centreville, Virginia. This is the approximate location of where the Marine Battalion camped for two days. The area would have been very rural with a small village located to the east. Upon completion of this Stop, return to Route 29 and drive approximately 1.5 miles west to Stop 3, Cub Run Bridge.

Historic marker at camp site of McDowell's Army. (Author's collection)

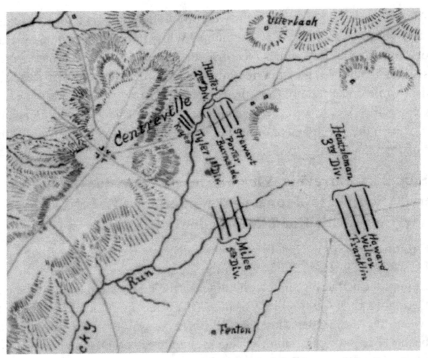

**Section of 1861 map depicting camp locations of the Army of Northeastern
Virginia, Second Division**

(Library of Congress Geography and Map Division Washington, D.C.)

Brigadier General Irvin McDowell, leading the Army of Northeastern
Virginia, planned his attack for the early morning of July 21. Colonel
Israel Richardson's brigade of the 1st Division, along with the brigade of
Colonel Thomas Davies of the 5th Division, would feint toward
Blackburn's Ford. The remaining three brigades of Brigadier General
Daniel Tyler's 1st Division would conduct a feint toward the Stone Bridge
on the Warrenton Turnpike. The remaining brigade of Colonel Dixon
Miles's 5th Division would remain as a reserve at Centreville. The main
body of troops would march north to maneuver around the Confederate
left flank.

**Brigadier General Irvin McDowell, commanding the Army of Northeastern
Virginia. (National Archives and Records Administration)**

The maneuver was assigned to the divisions of Colonel David Hunter and
Colonel Samuel Heintzelman. The plan called for Colonel Hunter's
division, to which the Marine Battalion was assigned, to cross Bull Run
Creek at Sudley Ford, while Colonel Heintzelman's Brigade would cross
at Poplar Ford to the Southeast. The two divisions would conduct a link-
up and then march south to the Warrenton Turnpike with the two brigades
abreast of each other.

**Col. David Hunter commanding the Second Division, Army
of Northeastern Virginia. (CDV by E Anthony of New York City)**

This complicated plan relied on two inexperienced brigades to conduct a forward passage of lines, followed by a night march of approximately two miles, to the bridge across the Cub Run, followed by a change of direction off the main service road onto an unimproved road that was described as a "cow path" for an unknown distance (thought to be two miles but was actually closer to five mile), followed by the conduct of a creek crossing at two separate locations. Once all of this was completed, the two brigades were to link up in the vicinity of the Sudley Road to begin offensive combat operations.

General McDowell ordered the march to begin at 0230 on the morning of July 21 and planned for Hunter's column to cross Sudley Ford by 0700. The march, however, did not go as planned. The following excerpt from Major of Engineers J. G. Barnard in his report to the Assistant Adjutant General dated 29 July 1861 describes the march: "You are aware of the unexpected delay. The two leading brigades of Tyler's had not cleared the road for Hunter to this point until half-past five, and our guide, alleging that a nearer route to the ford would bring our columns in sight of the enemy's batteries, led them by so circuitous a way that Hunter did not reach Sudley until half-past nine or thereabouts."

About 0200 on Sunday, July 21, units of McDowell's army began leaving their camps at Centreville to stage for the morning's march. From the start, the march was beset with delays. The 1st Brigade commander of the 2nd Division, Colonel Andrew Porter, described the decision for the Marine's assignment on the morning of July 21: "The Marines were recruits, but through constant exertions of their officers had been brought to a fine military appearance, without being able to render much active service. They were therefore attached to the battery [Griffin] as its permanent support." The order of march was set as follows: Griffin's Battery, Marine Battalion, 27th New York Volunteers, 14th New York State Militia, 8th New York State Militia, U.S. Infantry Battalion, and the U.S. Cavalry Battalion. Major Bartlett of the 27th New York noted in his official report of the battle, "At precisely 2 o'clock a.m. we formed for march in rear of the Marine Corps, commanded by Major Reynolds."

**Col. Andrew Porter, commanding 1ˢᵗ Brigade,
2ⁿᵈ Division, Army of Northeastern Virginia
(Matthew Brady Photo)**

Tyler's division moved onto the Warrenton Turnpike first, which delayed the movement of the flanking columns of Hunter and Heintzelman. Tyler, stung by his rebuke from McDowell two days earlier, took his time and moved cautiously westward. Traveling with Tyler's division was a 2½ - ton, 30-pounder Parrott rifle. When it arrived at the Cub Run Bridge, there was concern that the structure might not hold the gun's weight. The column halted while engineers reinforced the bridge, causing further delay. It was not until 0530 that the rear of Tyler's column finally crossed Cub Run Bridge, allowing Hunter and Heintzelman to cross and begin their march north toward Sudley and Poplar Fords. The two commanders discovered, however, that the route chosen by the engineers soon turned into a little-used footpath through the woods. With frequent halts to clear trees and brush, the column slowly worked its way northward.

Stop 3 – Cub Run Bridge – Route 29 and Cub Run

Orientation: The modern-day Cub Run Bridge is in approximately the same location as was the bridge of 1861. Modern day Route 29/Lee Highway, however, has greatly expanded, and the surrounding topography has been adjusted. It is suggested that you park on a nearby side street or frontage road due east of the bridge near Prince and Lee Highway. Proceed to the bridge area on foot to read the Civil War Trails marker. Lee Highway is a divided highway that runs east and west. The Cub Run bridge is approximately 3½ miles from the Sudley Road/Lee Highway intersection to the west.

Modern view of Cub Run Bridge along Lee Highway (Author's collection)

Background: At approximately 0530 hours on the morning of July 21, Porter's brigade, to which the Marine Battalion belonged, arrived at the Cub Run Bridge. Upon crossing the bridge, the column advanced a few hundred yards then turned north at a blacksmith shop and continued the march along a mere "cow path" through the Grigsby Farm. Today the route of march is long gone due to development and is now occupied by townhomes. The entrance to the "cow path" is in the vicinity of the eastern most portion of the Centreville Baptist Church, off Route 29. This is also the location of McDowell's temporary headquarters early on the morning of July 21.

Major Barnard described the delay:

> Accompanying the Commanding General, we, as you are aware, after waiting two or three hours at the turn-off, rode on to overtake the front of Hunter's division, when we emerged from the woods, nearly northeast of Sudley, into the open country, from whence the course of the run and the slopes of the opposite shore could be seen; we could perceive the enemy's column in motion to meet us. The loss of time here, in a great measure, thwarted our plan. We had hoped to pass the ford and reach the rear of the enemy's forces at Warrenton Stone Bridge before he could assemble in sufficient force to cope with us.

Stop 4 – Sudley Church

Orientation: Parking is available at the modern day Sudley Church, or in the small lot adjacent to the church near the interpretive markers. After parking, carefully cross Lee Highway on foot and proceed to the National Park Service gate entrance for the trail down to Sudley Springs Ford of Bull Run. After entering through the gate, follow the path to your left, which will lead down to the ford. Coordination with the Visitor Center on the Manassas National Battlefield Park may be needed to gain access through the gate.

Sudley Springs Ford crossing location
(Author's collection)

Notes: At about 0930 on July 21, hours behind schedule, the head of Hunter's column reached Sudley Ford. After a short halt to rest and replenish canteens the march resumed past the Sudley Church, where parishioners preparing for Sunday services stopped to stare at the passing column. McDowell soon joined the column and urged haste. Meanwhile, Heintzelman's division missed the road to the crossing at Poplar Ford and continued to follow Hunter. The result would be that both divisions would enter the battle one behind the other, rather than two abreast as the planned called for.

Leading Hunter's advance south from Sudley Ford was the brigade of Colonel Burnside. Burnside's command consisted of the 1st Rhode Island Infantry, 2nd Rhode Island Infantry, accompanied by the governor of Rhode Island, William Sprague. The 2nd New Hampshire Infantry and the 71st New York Infantry came with two 12-pounder boat howitzers borrowed from the Washington Navy Yard. Brigade artillery was Company A, 1st Rhode Island Light Artillery, commanded by Captain William Reynolds.

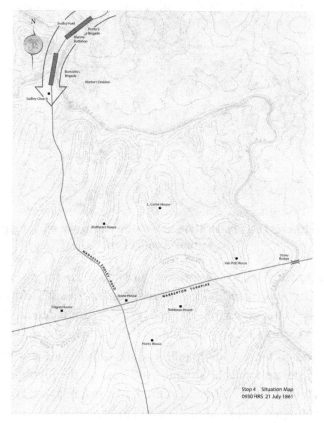

(Brian D. Wishner)

Stop 5 – Matthews Hill parking lot adjacent to Sudley Road, modern VA 234.

Orientation: Travel to Mathews Hill parking area and exit your vehicle. Move to the interpretive sign at the edge of the parking lot facing South East. Stops 4 and 5 will be conducted from this location. North is in the direction of the interpretive map in the parking lot as you are facing it. The Visitor Center is to the southeast, Warrenton Turnpike (US 29) and Sudley Road (VA 234) and is just below the hill, also to the southeast. Marine Barracks Washington is about 25 miles east. Dogan Ridge is the wooded high ground to the southwest overlooking the Stone House intersection of modern-day Route 29/234.

Matthews Hill observation area adjacent to the parking lot
(Author's collection)

At approximately 1030 Ambrose Burnside's command approached
Matthews Hill and came under fire from Nathan Evans's skirmishers on
the hill-rest. After a couple of volleys, the Confederate skirmishers
withdrew to Evans's main command on the southern slope.

The 2nd Division turned South and, leading with Burnside's 2nd Brigade,
began Confederate forces at around 1100, just on the high ground above
the Stone House. The 1st Brigade of the 2nd Division, to which the Marine
Battalion belonged, followed in trace and to the west/right.

Burnside deployed his brigade, and Reynolds's six, bronze 14-pounder
rifles unlimbered only 200 yards from Evans's line. The battery's right
rested on the Manassas-Sudley Road. Reynolds's guns quickly became
engaged with the two guns of the Lynchburg Artillery to the south.

While Burnside battled for Matthews Hill, Porter's brigade arrived behind
Burnside's line. Porter's command consisted of the 8th New York Infantry,
14th New York State Militia (known as the 14th Brooklyn), 27th New York
Infantry, Sykes's U.S. Infantry Battalion, the U.S. Marine Battalion, and a
U.S. Cavalry Battalion. Battery D, 5th U.S. Artillery, commanded by
Captain Charles Griffin, completed the brigade.

Col. G Lyons	Col. AM Wood	Col. HW Slocum	Maj. G Sykes
8th NY Militia	14th Brooklyn	27th New York	US Infantry Bn

Maj. JG Reynolds	Maj. IN Palmer	Capt. C Griffin
US Marine Bn	US Cavalry Bn	Co D 5th US Artillery

Shortly after Porter's first brigade arrived, the 2nd Division's commander, Colonel Hunter, was wounded and carried to the rear, telling Colonel Burnside of the 2nd Brigade, "I leave the matter in your hands."

At about 1100, the Staunton Virginia Artillery, commanded by Captain John Imboden arrived on the field and unlimbered his four six-pounder smoothbores in a depression about one hundred yards north of Henry House and opened long-range fire on the advancing Union forces.

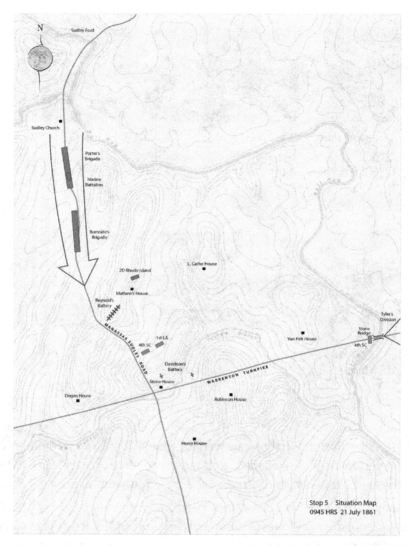

(Brian D. Wishner)

Stop 6 – View of Dogan Ridge –

Orientation: Dogan Ridge is not accessible by vehicle and must be observed from a distance or by crossing Sudley Road by foot. Proceed past the Matthews Hill interpretive marker along the grass trail until you reach the five bronze park service guns that marks the location of the 2nd Rhode

Island's James Rifles. North is the direction of the Matthews Hill parking lot. The area immediately in front of the James Rifles is known as "Buck Hill." To the southeast is the intersection of Sudley Road and the Warrenton Turnpike. The Marine Battalion was deployed in support of Griffin's Battery on the hillside across Sudley Road to the west. Most of the Marine position is now obscured by modern tree growth. Once you have completed with Stop 5, return to your vehicle and drive down to the Route 29/234 intersection Stone House parking area.

View of Dogan Ridge and the area where Griffin's Battery and the Marine Battalion were deployed. (Author's collection)

Notes: After McDowell arrived on Matthews Hill to take command, Porter extended the Union line to Dogan Ridge, west of the Manassas-Sudley Road. Griffin's six guns and six guns of Battery I, 1st U.S. Artillery (Franklin's brigade) unlimbered in front of Porter's line and opened fire on the distant Confederate forces. As Porter wrote in his official report, "Griffin's Battery found its way through the timber to the fields beyond, followed promptly by the Marines, while the Twenty-Seventh took direction more to the left."

"When we arrived," wrote Private William Barrett, "just as we got out of the woods in the rear of the battery, we lost three men by cannon balls."

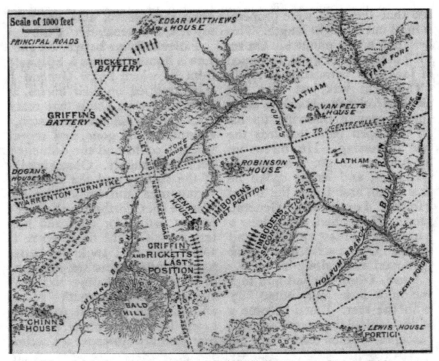

Map depicting the location of Griffin's Battery on Dogan Ridge
The Century, **30, May 1885. p. 95 (Library of Congress)**

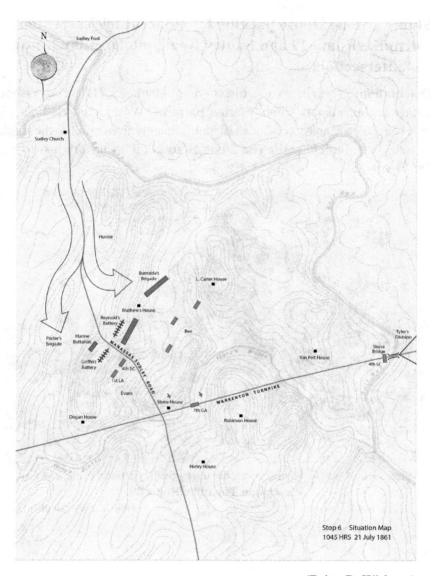

(Brian D. Wishner)

Stop 7 - Stone House parking lot adjacent to Warrenton Turnpike/Route 29 and Sudley Road, modern-day Route 234 intersection.

Orientation: North is in the direction of Matthews Hill. The Visitor Center is immediately south. Marine Barracks, Washington is about 25 miles east. The Manassas railhead is approximately fives miles to the south of today's battlefield park. The Stone House building is original to the 1861 battlefield.

Stone House at the corner of modern day Sudley Road/Route 234 and Warrenton Turnpike/Route 29.

(Author's collection)

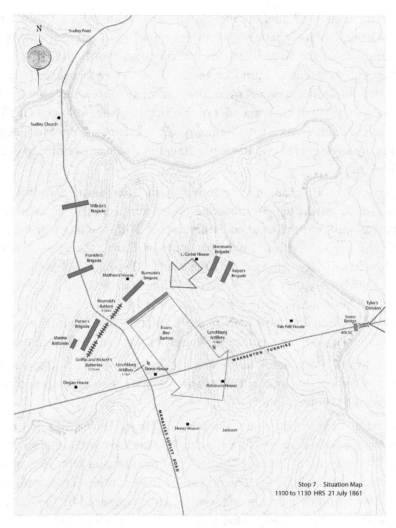

(Brian D. Wishner)

Notes: Union troops initially had success, pushing the Confederate troops off Matthews Hill. Captain Griffin's Battery was ordered to take up positions on the high ground, on the west side of the Sudley/Route 29. The 1st Brigade was ordered to take up positions to the rear of Griffin's guns, with the Marines being placed on the right flank. (See Stop 7 situation map).

Over the next two hours, as the Union Infantry drove the Confederate forces back, Griffin's battery would make a series of advances along the western side of the Sudley/29 Road to ridge just north and west of the Sudley and Warrenton Turnpike Intersection. At each pause, Griffin's guns would inflict severe casualties on the Confederate flank. The Marines, along with the remainder of the First Brigade, followed Griffin's guns at the double-quick (double-time). Up to this point, the Marines had yet to play any direct role in the battle other than losing three men to enemy artillery fire.

Burnside's 1st Brigade made another push after noon and this time managed to push the Confederate defenders across the Warrenton Turnpike and onto the crest of Henry House Hill, southeast of the road intersection. Just before 1400 hours, Major Barry, the commander of McDowell's artillery, appeared on the scene. He ordered Captain Griffin to take his battery and advance into position near the Henry House. The Assistant Adjutant General assigned to the 1st Brigade then ordered the Marine Battalion and the 11th New York Infantry Regiment (also part of the Second Brigade) to advance in support of Captain Griffin's battery.

Notes: Major Reynolds, seeing the horse drawn artillery had already moved off at a gallop, ordered the Marines to drop their bedrolls and move forward at the double-quick.

Proceed to Stop 8, just below the crest of Henry House Hill and to the northeast of the modern Visitor Center. Use the crosswalk intersection to cross the Warrenton Turnpike/Route 234 if traveling on foot. Be watchful of traffic as the volume of vehicles can be high at times. Once across the road, use the following map and use the same path used by the Marines. You will again be walking in the footsteps of the Marines of '61.

Stop 8 – Marine Battalion Marker, Henry House Hill

Orientation: North is in the direction of Stone House. The Visitor Center is immediately southeast, Washington and the Marine Barracks are to the east. The Henry House is immediately adjacent to the marker, the Manassas railhead that is approximately four miles beyond today's battlefield park to the south.

The Marines of 61 marker on Henry House Hill (Author's collection)

Notes: The Marine Battalion was positioned in a linear formation on the low ground immediately behind Griffin's artillery battery and the Henry House. The battery had already unlimbered and commenced firing by the time the Marine Battalion caught up. The battalion was still assigned as the infantry support for Griffin's battery. The only other Union infantry on Henry House Hill were the 11th New York and 1st Minnesota, but they were positioned on the far-right flank, just to the right rear of Ricketts's Battery. The Marine Battalion had no flank support and could not see what was going on in the fight to its immediate front. Recall that this was the first time 95 percent of the battalion's personnel had been in combat. To complicate matters further, there was no standard uniform for the Union and Confederate Armies at that time. Telling friend from foe, with smoke covering battlefield, was a challenge.

Major Reynolds ordered the Marines to lie down to avoid unnecessary exposure to fire and provide the men a chance to catch their breath after running from past the Stone House to their present location. The raw Marines had kept good order but were physically drained after running to keep up with the quick moving artillery. It is believed that Captain Griffin requested the Marines to move further south, along the ridge, to protect the exposed guns on the right of the line. Captain Griffin had just ordered Lieutenant Henry Hasbrouck's section of artillery, two twelve-pound howitzers, to move to the far right of the line past Ricketts's battery and thus protect the Union right flank. Once the Marines had shifted positions, a few Marine officers moved forward to observe the artillery fire, just 400 yards to their front, and to get a better assessment of the situation. One of these officers, Lieutenant Robert Hitchcock of Company C, remarked, "the cannon balls are flying pretty thick." Just afterwards, a cannon ball ricocheted off the ground immediately in front of Hitchcock. The solid shot ball leapt forward and decapitated the young lieutenant. As Hitchcock's body fell, one of his Marines attempted to catch him. A second ball took off the Marine's arm and severed Hitchcock's lifeless body.

**Area of low ground behind Griffin's Battery where Marines first deployed
on Henry House Hill (Author's collection)**

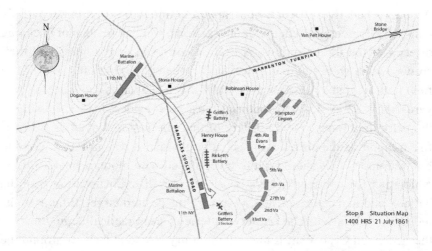

(Brian D. Wishner)

Stop 9 – Captain James Rickets Gun Line, Henry House Hill

Orientation: North is in the direction of Stone House. The Visitor Center is immediately south. Washington and the Marine Barracks are about 25 miles east. Griffin's and Ricketts's batteries are to your immediate front. The Confederate main line is just opposite the high ground to your front and just out of line of site. The Henry House is immediately adjacent left section of the replicated battery. The Marine Battalion is positioned just beyond the battery in the low ground between the battery and Route 234/Sudley Road.

To understand the footprint of a six-gun battery and the tactical integrity of that battery as it was employed at Manassas, we must understand that battery's table of organization. A standard field artillery battery consisted of six guns. Each gun was attached to a limber, pulled by six horses, which served as the primary mover. Each gun was supported by a caisson, also attached to a limber pulled by six horses. The caisson carried two ammunition chests and a spare wheel. There was one chest on each limber for a total of about 960 rounds for the battery. There were also a battery wagon, a forge wagon, and an ambulance, for a total of eighteen vehicles.

A battery had five officers: one captain commanding the battery of six guns, one lieutenant in charge of the caissons, and one lieutenant in charge of each of the three sections. A section consisted of two guns and their crews, which were referred to as "left," "center," and "right." In 1861, a field battery of six guns had a ground width of 82 yards and a depth of 45 yards. This 82-by-45-yard footprint must be considered when looking at the battlefield today. Field artillery of that era was employed as a direct-fire weapon. If the crews could see a target, and it was in range, it could be fired upon. This should not to be confused with modern field artillery, which can fire indirectly, have observers at a different location than the battery, and in most cases, never even see the desired target. Infantry units did not intermix with the artillery batteries during tactical deployment in the American Civil War. Rather, the infantry would maneuver around the batteries, thus permitting continuous fire to be maintained by the guns. Intermixing units would degrade not only tactical integrity but also command and control.

Captain Griffin's battery, Light Company D of the 5th US artillery, nicknamed the "West Point Battery," consisted of six guns (four ten-pound Parrot Rifles and two twelve-pound Field Howitzers)

ten-pound Parrot Rifle   twelve-pound Field Howitzer

(Author's collection)

**A Federal Light battery of six guns "limbered up" and ready to move
(James F. Gibson, Library of Congress)**

**Battery D 2nd US Artillery "deployed" at Fredericksburg June 1863
(Timothy O' Sullivan, Library of Congress)**

Shortly after Hitchcock's death, Confederate troops advanced from across the field toward Griffin's newly positioned guns. Griffin ordered his men to load canister and engage the enemy. Unfortunately, McDowell's artillery chief, Major William Barry, countermanded the order to fire. He informed Griffin that "the men he sees approaching are his infantry support" and to not fire upon them. The charging troops were clad in blue

uniforms, but they belonged to the 33rd Virginia Infantry under
"Stonewall" Jackson's command. The Virginians approached Griffin's
two guns unmolested and delivered a devastating volley at 70 yards into
the cannoneers. "Yelling like savages," the Virginia troops charged the
guns and routed the remaining crews. While the 33rd Virginia was taking
Griffin's right section of guns, Colonel J. E. B. Stuart's 1st Virginia
Cavalry charged the right flank of the 11th New York Infantry.

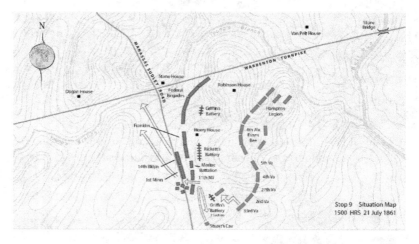

(Brian D. Wishner)

Col. Stuart saw the retreating regiments of the 1st Minnesota and 11th New
York. The 1st Minnesota was uniformed in black hats and trousers with red
shirts. The 11th New York, the so-called "Fire Zouaves," were outfitted in
blue trousers, red shirts, gray jackets, and red kepis. Believing these men
to be fellow Confederates, Stuart rode out among them shouting, "Don't
run boys – we are here!" He was ignored by the red-shirted New Yorkers
but soon noticed the stars and stripes as it unfurled in the breeze. Stuart
wheeled his horse around and quickly returned to the awaiting squadrons
of the 1st Virginia.

Stuart ordered the 1st Virginia forward toward the retreating Union troops.
Within 50 yards of contact, the 11th New York attempted to form and repel
the mounted assault. The Fire Zouaves leveled muskets and unleashed a
ragged volley. Casualties among the 1st Virginia were minimal, but the

smoke of the muskets screened any telling signs from the eyes of the New York. The Union troops reeled from the charge and sought immediate cover from nearby woods just west of Sudley Road. Although Stuart's attack did little damage to the Union force, it had come at just the right time and effectively ended the battle for both the 1st Minnesota and 11th New York as organized units.

The Marine Battalion, now for the most part the only organized Union force on Henry Hill, retuned fire at the advancing Confederates as retreating Union solders streamed past them. The advancing Virginians now focused volley fires on the Marine Battalion. Confederate gunners also targeted the lone, organized remaining Union unit on Henry Hill. The Marines began to take heavy casualties from the front and flank from the combined enemy fire. To complicate matters, retreating troops began to get intermingled in the Marine formation. With the Marine Battalion "caught up" in the general stampede back to the crossroads, Major Reynolds ordered the remaining Marines to fall back.

Proceed to the next stop located just on the far side of Visitor Center parking lot.

Marine line preparing to fire - (USMCHC)

Stop 10 – Griffin's single section of guns on the right of the Federal Line

Orientation: North is the high ground opposite Warrenton Turnpike/Route 29, The Visitor Center is now immediately to the north. Your current location is at Griffin's 2 guns opposite the Henry House and Ricketts battery in between the Visitor Center parking lot and the Confederate line. The Confederate main line is now clearly visible to the east running southwest to northeast.

The Marine Battalion was in a state of self-preservation. Unit cohesion no longer existed; the battalion had suffered significant casualties. Some men were missing, having been caught up in a general "stampede" from the field. The Marines rallied and reformed near the crossroads and, with the reorganized 14th Brooklyn Regiment and the 79th New York, advanced back up the hill to retake the captured Union guns. Cresting the hill near the remnants of Ricketts's Battery, the two infantry regiments and Marine Battalion began to deliver enfilade fire. The three Union units continued to advance in a column of regiments with the 14th Brooklyn in the lead, followed by the Marine Battalion and, lastly, the 79th New York.

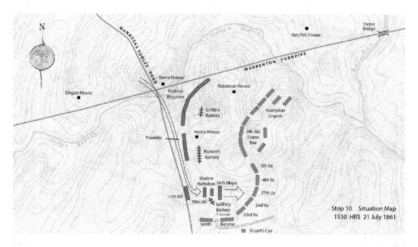

(Brian D. Wishner)

At this point in the staff ride, you may follow the route of the final Marine assault on the Confederate line. Approach the Confederate line in the footsteps of the Marines of '61. The three units deployed on line and continued to advance through a pine thicket and toward the Confederate line. As enemy fire intensified, the 79th New York regiment broke and began to fall back towards the crossroads from which they came. The two remaining units advanced to within 50 yards of the Confederate line when the 14th Brooklyn went to ground to avoid a volley from Jackson's line. The Marine Battalion took the brunt of the volley as it was now completely exposed and the only viable target. The Marine Battalion passed through the 14th Brooklyn and continued its advance, piercing Jackson's line. Alone and unsupported, the Marine line was forced back and began to fall apart as remnants of the 14th Brooklyn became intermingled with the Marines.

Surgeon Daniel M. Conrad of the 2nd Virginia Infantry surveyed the bloody aftermath and would later remark, "the green pines were filled with the 79th Highlanders and the red-breeched Brooklyn Zouaves, but the only men that were killed and wounded twenty to thirty yards behind and in the rear of our lines were the United States Marines."

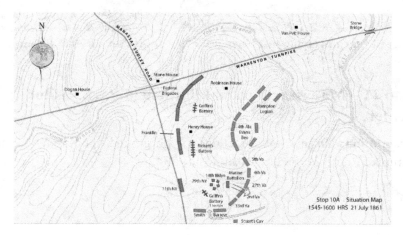

(Brian D. Wishner)

**Dead Marines laying just beyond the line of the 2nd Virginia Infantry,
(USMCHC)**

Stop 11 – Manassas National Battlefield Park Visitor Center

Orientation: North is the direction of high ground opposite Warrenton Turnpike/Route 29, Sudley Road/ Route 234.

Manassas National Battlefield Park Visitor's Center (Author)

The second repulse of the Marine Battalion was significant. The Marines were beyond the crossroads before Major Reynolds could halt and reform the battalion. For a second time, Major Reynolds was able to reform the battalion and move to the vicinity of the crossroads. The battalion then pushed up the Sudley Newmarket road, using the high ground to mask its movements. They then took up a position on the reverse slope of Henry House Hill along with other units of the Army. Union Army regiments again formed for another assault, and the Marine Battalion joined in on the advance. As the Union Regiments advanced, Confederate reinforcements entered the field and began firing volleys into the advancing Union regiments' flank. The army regiments, along with the Marine Battalion, withdrew to the protection of the roadbed and fell back down the road towards the intersection. There the broken units began to reform yet again.

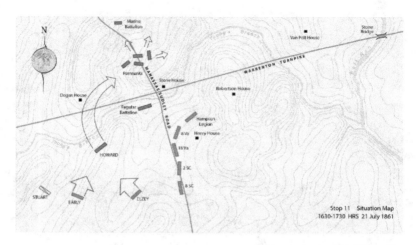

(Brian D. Wishner)

As the regiments broken from the fighting on Henry Hill were reforming, the Union left broke under the pressure of an all-out Confederate attack. This time there was no stopping the Union retreat, which fled back in the direction of Washington. The Marines initially fell back in good order, even forming a rear guard for a short period.

The disorganized and demoralized Union Army spent a miserable rainy night winding its way back to Washington. Major Reynolds arrived at the Long Bridge on the outskirts of Washington and found a large body of soldiers and about 70 Marines held from crossing the Potomac by the Provost Guard. Reynolds's pride in his Corps and compassion for his men compelled him to persuade the Provost Officer to allow his Marines to cross, and he marched them back to Marine Barracks, Washington.

Losses to the Marine Battalion included nine dead, nineteen wounded, and thirteen missing. Commandant Harris noted this as an embarrassment to the Corps: "it is the first instance in recorded history where its members were forced to turn their backs to the enemy." Whether he was making a political statement about his displeasure over Marines serving under Army command, or being kept out of the planning process by the Secretary of Navy, will continue to be disputed for years to come. Despite their losses, Colonel Andrew Porter, commanding the brigade to which the Marine Battalion belonged, would praise the Marines for their performance in his after action report, stating that although they were recruits, "through constant exertions of their officers [they] had been brought to a fine military appearance." Throughout the remainder of the war, the Marines would be involved in numerous amphibious operations along the southern coasts, but they would never again serve in major operations under the command of the U.S. Army.

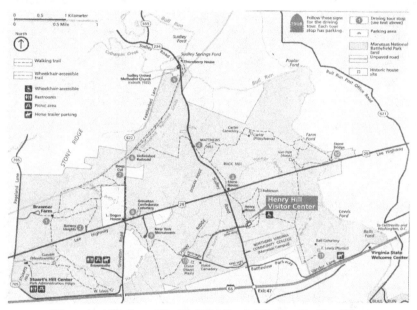

Manassas National Battlefield Park Visitor Center Map
(National Park Service)

QUESTIONS FOR CRITICAL THOUGHT ON THE BATTLE OF 1st MANASSAS

1. What role did small unit leadership play during the deployment of and subsequent actions by Marines on the battlefield at 1st Manassas?

2. Do you agree with the decision of Colonel Andrew Porter to assign the Marine Battalion in "direct support" of a battery of Federal artillery? If so, why? If not, why not?

3. What factors led to the success of the Marine Battalion being the only Federal unit to pierce Brigadier General Thomas J. "Stonewall" Jackson's line on Henry House Hill?

4. After the battle, Major Reynolds met "his Marines" at Long Bridge, as they returned to Washington. What message do you believe was conveyed by his actions at Long Bridge?

5. Having read this book, what message was Marine Corps Commandant John Harris sending with his statement that this was an embarrassment to our Corps as "it is the first instance in recorded history where its members were forced to turn their backs to the enemy?"

The Marine Battalion Order of Battle, July 21, 1861

Major John George Reynolds, Commanding

Staff

Major Augustus S. Nicholson, Adjutant

Major William S. Slack, Quartermaster

Sergeant Major (name unknown)

Quartermaster Sergeant Smith Maxwell

Company A

Brevet Major Jacob Zeilen, Commanding

Second Lieutenant Frank Munroe

Second Lieutenant John H. Grimes

Company B

Captain James H. Jones, Commanding

Second Lieutenant Robert W. Huntington

Company C

First Lieutenant Alan Ramsay, Commanding

Second Lieutenant Robert E. Hitchcock

Company D

Second Lieutenant William H. Cartter, Commanding

Second Lieutenant William H. Hale

Twelve Officers

Two Non-commissioned staff officers

Four First Sergeants

Three Second Sergeants

Eight Corporals

Three Musicians

One apprentice music boy

320 privates (approx.)

Aggregate Battalion Strength: approximately 353

Report of Colonel Andrew Porter,
16ᵗʰ U.S. Infantry, commanding 1ˢᵗ Brigade, 2ⁿᵈ Division

July 16-22, 1861 – The Bull Run, or Manassas, Campaign

HDQRS. FIRST BRIGADE, SECOND DIVISION,
Arlington, Va., July 25, 1861

Brig. and Div. Capt. J. B. FRY,
Assistant Adjutant-General.

SIR: I have the honor to submit the following account of the operations of the First Brigade, Second Division, of the Army, in the battle before Manassas, on the 21st instant. The brigade was silently paraded in light marching order at 2 o'clock in the morning of that day, composed as follows, viz: Griffin's battery; marines, Major Reynolds; Twenty-seventh New York Volunteers, Colonel Slocum; Fourteenth New York State Militia, Colonel Wood; Eighth New York State Militia, Colonel Lyons; battalion regulars, Major Sykes; one company Second Dragoons, two companies First Cavalry, four companies Second Cavalry, Major Palmer. Total strength, 3,700. The marines were recruits, but through the constant exertions of their officers had been brought to present a fine military appearance, without being able to render much active service. They were therefore attached to the battery as its permanent support through the day.

Owing to frequent delays in the march of troops in front, the brigade did not reach Centreville until 4.30 a.m., and it was an hour after sunrise when the head of it was turned to the right to commence the flank movement. The slow and intermittent movements of the Second Brigade (Burnside's) were then followed through the woods for four hours, which brought the head of our division to Bull Run and Sudley's Mill, where a halt of half an hour took place, to rest and refresh the men and horses. From the heights on this side of the run a vast column of the enemy could be plainly descried, at the distance of a mile or more on our left, moving rapidly towards our line of march in front. Some disposition of skirmishers was then directed to be made at the head of the Column by the division commander, in which Colonel Slocum, of the Second Rhode Island Regiment, was observed to bear an active part. The column moved forward, however, before they were completed, and in about thirty minutes emerged from the timber, when the rattle of musketry and occasional crash of round shot through the leaves and branches of the trees in our vicinity betokened the opening of battle.

The head of the brigade was immediately turned slightly to the right, in order to gain time and room for deployment on the right of the Second Brigade. Griffin's battery found its way through the timber to the fields beyond, followed promptly by the marines, while the Twenty-seventh took direction more to the left, and the Fourteenth followed upon the trail of the battery, all moving up at a double-quick step. The enemy appeared drawn up in a long line, extending along the Warrenton turnpike from a house and haystacks upon our extreme right to a house beyond the left of the division. Behind that house there was a heavy masked battery, which, with three others along his line on the heights beyond, covered the ground upon which we were advancing with all sorts of projectiles. A grove in front of his right wing afforded it shelter and protection, while the shrubbery along the road, with fences, screened somewhat his left wing. Griffin advanced to within a thousand yards and opened a deadly and unerring fire upon his batteries, which were soon silenced or driven away. Our right was rapidly developed by the marines, Twenty-seventh, Fourteenth, and Eighth, with the cavalry in rear of the right, the enemy retreating with more precipitation than order as our line advanced.

The Second Brigade (Burnside's) was at this time attacking the enemy's right with, perhaps, too hasty vigor. The enemy clung to the protecting wood with great tenacity, and the Rhode Island Battery became so much endangered as to impel the commander of the Second Brigade to call for the assistance of the battalion of regulars. At this time I received the information through Capt. W. D. Whipple, A. A. G., that Colonel Hunter was seriously wounded, and had directed him to report to me as commander of the division; and in reply to the urgent request of Colonel Burnside, I detached the battalion of regulars to his assistance. For an account of its operations I would respectfully beg a reference to the enclosed report of its commander, Major Sykes [No. 35].

The rebels soon come flying from the woods towards the right, and the Twenty-seventh completed their rout by charging directly upon their center in the face of a scorching fire, while the Fourteenth and Eighth moved down the turnpike to cut off the retiring foe, and to support the Twenty-seventh, which had lost its gallant colonel, but was standing the brunt of the action, with its ranks thinning in the dreadful fire. Now the resistance of the enemy's left was so obstinate that the beaten right retired in safety.

The head of Heintzelman's column at this moment appeared upon the field, and the Eleventh and Fifth Massachusetts Regiments moved forward to the support of our center, while staff officers could be seen galloping rapidly in every direction, endeavoring to rally the broken Eighth; but this laudable purpose was only partially attained, owing to the inefficiency of some of its field officers.

The Fourteenth, though it had broken, was soon rallied in rear of Griffin's battery, which soon took up a position farther to the front and right, from which his fire was delivered with such precision and rapidity as to compel the batteries of the enemy to retire in consternation far behind the brow of the hill in front. At this time, my brigade occupied a line considerably in advance of that first occupied by the left wing of the enemy. The battery was pouring its withering fire into the batteries and columns of the enemy whenever they exposed themselves. The cavalry was engaged in feeling the left flank of the enemy's positions, in doing which some important captures were made--one by Sergeant Sacks, of the Second Dragoons, of a General George Steuart, of Baltimore. Our cavalry also emptied the saddles of several the mounted rebels.

General Tyler's division was engaged with the enemy's right. The Twenty-seventh was resting in the edge of the woods, in the center, covered by a hill, upon which lay the Eleventh and Fifth Massachusetts, occasionally delivering a scattering fire. The Fourteenth was moving to the right flank. The Eighth had lost its organization. The marines were moving up in fine style in rear of the Fourteenth, and Captain Arnold was occupying a height on the middle ground with his battery. At this juncture there was a temporary lull in the firing from the rebels, who appeared only occasionally on the heights in irregular formations, but to serve as marks for Griffin's guns.

The prestige of success had thus far attended the efforts of our inexperienced, but gallant, troops. The lines of the enemy had been forcibly shifted nearly a mile to their left and rear. The flags of eight regiments, though borne somewhat wearily, now pointed towards the hill from which disordered masses of rebels had been seen hastily retiring.

Griffin's and Ricketts' batteries were ordered by the commanding general to the top of the hill on our right, supporting them with Fire Zouaves and marines, while the Fourteenth entered the skirt of woods on their right, to protect that flank, and a column, composed of the Twenty-seventh New York, Eleventh and Fifth Massachusetts, First Minnesota, and Sixty ninth New York, moved up towards the left flank of the batteries; but so soon as they were in position, and before the flanking supports had reached theirs, a murderous fire of musketry and rifles, opened at pistol range, cut down every cannoneer and a large number of horses. The fire came from some infantry of the enemy, which had been mistaken for our own forces, an officer on the field having stated that it was a regiment sent by Colonel Heintzelman to support the batteries.

The evanescent courage of the zouaves prompted them to fire perhaps a hundred shots, when they broke and fled, leaving the batteries open to a charge of the enemy's cavalry, which took place immediately. The marines also, in spite of the exertions of their gallant officers, gave way in disorder; the Fourteenth on the right and the column on the left hesitatingly retired, with the exception of the Sixty-ninth and Thirty-eighth New York, who nobly stood and returned the fire of the enemy for fifteen minutes. Soon the slopes behind us were swarming with our retreating and disorganized forces, whilst riderless horses and artillery teams ran furiously through the flying crowd. All further efforts were futile; the words, gestures, and threats of our officers were thrown away upon men who had lost all presence of mind and only longed for absence of body. Some of our noblest and best officers lost their lives in trying to rally them.

Upon our first position the Twenty-seventh was the first to rally, under the command of Major Bartlett, and around it the other regiments engaged soon collected their scattered fragments. The battalion of regulars, in the meantime, moved steadily across the held from the left to the right, and took up a position where it held the entire forces of the rebels in check until our forces were somewhat rallied. The commanding general then ordered a retreat upon Centreville, at the same time directing me to cover it with the battalion of regulars, the cavalry, and a section of artillery. The rear guard thus organized followed our panic-stricken people to Centreville, resisting the attacks of the rebel cavalry and artillery, and saving them from the inevitable destruction which awaited them had not this body been interposed.

Among those who deserve especial mention I beg leave to place the following names, viz:

Captain Griffin, for his coolness and promptitude in action, and for the handsome manner in which he handled his battery. Lieutenant Ames, of the same battery, who, after being wounded, gallantly served with it in action, and being unable to ride on horseback, was helped on and off a caisson in changes of position.

Captain Tillinghast, A. Q. M., who was ever present where his services were needed, carrying orders, rallying troops, and serving with the batteries, and finally, I have to state with the deepest sorrow, was mortally wounded.

Major Sykes and the officers of his command, three of whom (Lieutenants Latimer, Dickinson, and Kent) were wounded, who by their discipline, steadiness, and heroic fortitude, gave *éclat* to our attacks upon the enemy, and averted the dangers of a final overthrow.

Major Palmer and the cavalry officers under him, who by their daring intrepidity made the effectiveness of that corps all that it could be upon such a field in supporting batteries, feeling the enemy's position, and covering our retreat.

Major Reynolds, marines, whose zealous efforts were well sustained by his subordinates, two of whom, Brevet Major Zeilin and Lieutenant Hale, were wounded, and one, Lieutenant Hitchcock, lost his life.

Col. H. W. Slocum, who was wounded while leading his gallant Twenty-seventh New York to the charge, and Maj. J. J. Bartlett, who subsequently commanded it, and by his enthusiasm and valor kept it in action and out of the panic. His conduct was imitated by his subordinates, of whom two, Capt. H. C. Rodgers and Lieut. H. C. Jackson, were wounded, and one, Ensign Asa Park, was killed.

In the last attack Col. A.M. Wood, of the Fourteenth New York State Militia, was wounded, together with Captains R. B. Jordan and C. F. Baldwin, and Lieuts. J. A. Jones, T. R. Salter, R. A. Goodenough, and C. Scholes, and Adjutant Laidlaw.

The officers of the Fourteenth, especially Maj. James Jourdan, were distinguished by their display of spirit and efficiency throughout the action.

Surg. Charles C. Keeney, of the medical department, who by his professional skill, promptitude, and cheerfulness made the condition of the wounded of the Second Division comparatively comfortable. (He was assisted to a great extent by Dr. Rouch, of Chicago, a citizen.)

During the entire engagement I received extremely valuable aid and assistance from my aides-de-camp, Lieuts. C. F. Trowbridge and F. M. Bache, both of the Sixteenth Infantry.

Lieut. J. B. Howard, Fourteenth New York State Militia, A. A. Q. M. for the brigade, who by zealous attention to his duties succeeded in safely bringing the wagons of my brigade to Arlington.

The staff officers of the Second Division commander, via, Capt. W. D. Whipple, Lieutenants Cross and Flagler, served with me after the fall of Colonel Hunter, and I am indebted to them for gallant, faithful services during the day. Captain Whipple had his horse killed under him by a cannon ball.

Acting Asst. Adjt. General Lieut. W. W. Averell sustained the high reputation he had before won for himself as a brave and skillful officer, and to him I am very greatly indebted for aid and assistance, not only in performing with the greatest promptitude the duties of his position, but by exposing himself most fearlessly in rallying and leading forward the troops, he contributed largely to their general effectiveness against the enemy. I desire to call the attention of the commanding general particularly to him.

In conclusion, I beg leave to submit the enclosed return of killed, wounded, and missing in my brigade. Since the above reports were handed in many of the missing have returned, perhaps one-third of those reported. The enclosed report of Colonel Burnside, [No. 39], commanding Second

Brigade, was sent to me after the above report was written. While respectfully calling the attention of the general commanding to it, I would also ask leave to notice some misconceptions under which the colonel commanding the Second Brigade seems to have labored at the time of writing his report, viz: Of his agency in the management or formation of the Second Division, on the field; 2d, of the time that his brigade was entirely out of the action, with the exception of the New Hampshire Regiment; 3d, of the position of his brigade in the retreat, and particularly of the position of the Seventy-first New York, as he may have mistaken the rear guard, organized under my direction by your orders, for the enemy.

Captain Arnold's battery and the cavalry were directed and placed in their positions by my senior staff officer up to the time when Colonel Heintzelman ordered the cavalry to the front of the column.

Very respectfully, your obedient servant,
A. PORTER,
Colonel Sixteenth Infantry, U. S. Army, Comdg

APPENDIX A

A Letter from a Marine who was at Bull's Run

Pvt. William Barrett, U.S. Marine Battalion - 1861

I was in the fight at Manassas Gap or Bull's Run, as it may be called. The place has two names, but I think Bull's Run is the right one, by the way they treated us there. Out of our band of 320 marines that entered the field we only brought about 150 home with us. We were the first called to assist the Sixty-ninth. We faced them on the left of the battery, and when about fifty yards from it our men fell like hail stones. I had only fired three shots when my musket received a ball right at the lock, which put me back about three feet. As soon as I came to my ground again two men were shot down on my right and one on my left; about this time, I began to look very warlike. As for my part I thought I would lose all presence of mind in such a place, but it was quite different; I was as cool as a cucumber. Then we got orders to retreat and the Sixty-ninth and Ellsworth Zouaves played on them again. This was the time they suffered; they only stood a few minutes when they retreated without orders. Then we were again called on to face the enemy, fifty thousand strong, while we had only about 200. This time we got the Seventy-First to relieve us, but to no purpose; we had to retreat. Then it was a general retreat all round; everyone looked out for himself, but they took the short road and caught us again. If you had seen us swimming across Bull's Run, you would have thought there was something after us then. We had to come to Washington, forty-five miles, in our wet clothes, which were badly used up.

The route we took in going to Manassas Gap was by Arlington Heights and thence by Fairfax Court House, where several batteries had been erected. This was the first time we knew we had to fight; they never told us where we were going till then. When we were about a mile from the place, they got us to load our muskets. We were the first up to the battery, where we were drawn up in line of battle, when we found that the rebels had fled to Manassas. Then the cavalry was sent in hot pursuit of the enemy but failed to overtake them. We camped in Fairfax that night, and the boys enjoyed themselves by burning down the houses of the secessionists. Next morning, we took the march again, and went to Centreville by night; here we encamped two days.

On Monday morning at three o'clock we marched to the field, and as well as I can mind it was ten or eleven o'clock when we got there. It then looked very hot. The Seventy-first was the only regiment then at them. When we arrived, just as we got out of the woods in the rear of the battery, we lost three men by cannon balls. I could not describe to you what the battlefield looked like. At the time of the retreat we ran over the dead and wounded for a mile from the battery and to hear the wounded crying for help would have made the heart of stone ache. All along the road we had men, only wounded a little, who, when the long march came, had to give out and lie down to die. For ten miles this side of the field they could be seen lying here and there on the roadside.

Only four or five of the Pittsburgh boys, that I know of, were killed. One young fellow, named Frank Harris, who joined the Irish volunteers in Pittsburgh, was my right-hand man; going up to the battery he did not fire a single shot; he was one of the first to fall.

There were but few of the marines who were not wounded. I believe there are not thirty in the barracks who are not wounded more or less. I think they intended to fix me when they hit the lock of my musket. You could hear the ball playing "Yankee Doodle" around your ears but could not move. It was about as hot a place as I ever want to be in. I saw a horse's head taken off by a cannon ball at the time of our retreat; but he kept on ten or twelve yards before he found out that he was dead, then dropped and the poor fellow that was on his back had to take the hard road for it.

I cannot tell you any more about the battle at present, as I am very tired, have not slept any for forty-eight hours and marched from forty to fifty miles, fighting our way. I wish you would send me a Pittsburgh paper with an account of the battle, that I can see the difference in it.

W. B.

APPENDIX B

Report of Major John G. Reynolds,
Commanding Battalion of U.S. Marines

MARINE BARRACKS HEADQUARTERS,
Washington, July 24, 1861

CAPTAIN: I have the honor to report the movements and operations of the battalion of marines under my command detailed to co-operate with the Army.

The battalion left the barracks at headquarters in time to reach the Virginia end of the Potomac Long Bridge at 3 p.m. July 16, and proceeded up the Columbia turnpike until an officer, purporting to be the assistant adjutant-general of Colonel Porter's brigade, came up and assigned us position in the line of march, which placed us immediately in the rear of Captain Griffin's battery of flying artillery. This assignment was continued up to the period of the battle at Bull Run.

On reaching the field, and for some hours previously, the battery's accelerated march was such as to keep my command more or less in double-quick time; consequently, the men became fatigued or exhausted in strength. Being obliged at this period to halt, in order to afford those in the rear an opportunity of closing up and taking their proper place in line, the battery was lost to protection from the force under my command. This I stated to Colonel Porter, who was ever present, watching the events of the day. The position of the battery was pointed out, and I was directed to afford the necessary support. In taking this position the battalion was exposed to a galling fire. Whilst holding it, General McDowell ordered the battalion to cover or support the Fourteenth New York Regiment which was about to be engaged. The battalion, in consequence, took the position indicated by the general, but was unable to hold it, owing to the heavy fire which was opened upon them. They broke three several times, but as frequently formed, and urged back to their position, where finally a general rout took place, in which the marines participated. No effort on the part of their officers could induce them to rally.

I am constrained to call your attention to the fact that, when taking into consideration the command was composed entirely of recruits–not one being in service over three weeks, and many had hardly learned their facings, the officers likewise being but a short time in the service–their conduct was such as to elicit only the highest commendation.

Of the three hundred and fifty officers and enlisted men under my command, there were but two staff officers, two captains, one first lieutenant, and nine non-commissioned officers and two musicians who were experienced from length of service. The remainder were, of course, raw recruits, which being considered, I am happy to report the good conduct of officers and men. The officers, although but little experienced, were zealous in their efforts to carry out my orders.

In the death of Lieutenant Hitchcock, the corps has been deprived of a valuable acquisition. On the field he was ever present and zealous. He sought and won the approbation of his commanding and brother officers.

Enclosed please find a return of the battalion, showing its present strength, with casualties, &c.(*)

The abrupt and hasty retreat from the field of battle presents a deplorable deficiency in both arms and equipment.

The rout being of such a general character, the men of all arms commingled, the only alternative left was to hasten to the ground occupied by the brigade to which we were attached on the morning of the day of the battle. On my way thither I had the good fortune to fall in with General Meigs, whose consternation at the disastrous retreat was depicted upon his countenance. He was of the opinion the Army should hasten to Arlington, fearing otherwise the enemy would follow up their successes and cut us off on the road. My men being weary and much exhausted, without blankets and other necessaries, I determined to strengthen such as should pass the wagons by hot coffee, and move on to headquarters at Washington City, where their wants could be supplied. But few came up;

others continued on to the Long Bridge, where, on my arrival, I found some seventy or more, who, at my urgent solicitation, were permitted to accompany me to the barracks. In assuming the responsibility of the return to headquarters, I trust my course will meet the approbation of authority.

Blankets were thrown aside by my order on entering the field, which from force of circumstances we were afterwards unable to recover. All of which is respectfully.

I am, sir, very respectfully, your obedient servant,

JNO. GEO. REYNOLDS, Major, Commanding Battalion Marines

Capt. W. W. AVERELL,
A. A. A. G., First Brigade, Second Division, Arlington

APPENDIX C

*Report of Col. Andrew Porter, Sixteenth U. S. Infantry, commanding
Second Division and First Brigade, Second Division.
JULY 16-22, 1861. --The Bull Run, or Manassas, Campaign, Virginia.*

HDQRS. FIRST BRIGADE, SECOND DIVISION,
Arlington, Va., July 25, 1861.

Brig. and Div. Capt. J. B. FRY,
Assistant Adjutant-General.

*SIR: I have the honor to submit the following account of the operations of
the First Brigade, Second Division, of the Army, in the battle before
Manassas, on the 21st instant. The brigade was silently paraded in light
marching order at 2 o'clock in the morning of that day, composed as
follows, viz: Griffin's battery; marines, Major Reynolds; Twenty-seventh
New York Volunteers, Colonel Slocum; Fourteenth New York State
Militia, Colonel Wood; Eighth New York State Militia, Colonel Lyons;
battalion regulars, Major Sykes; one company Second Dragoons, two
companies First Cavalry, four companies Second Cavalry, Major Palmer.
Total strength, 3,700. The marines were recruits, but through the constant
exertions of their officers had been brought to present a fine military
appearance, without being able to render much active service. They were
therefore attached to the battery as its permanent support through the day.*

*Owing to frequent delays in the march of troops in front, the brigade did
not reach Centreville until 4.30 a.m., and it was an hour after sunrise when
the head of it was turned to the right to commence the flank movement.
The slow and intermittent movements of the Second Brigade (Burnside's)
were then followed through the woods for four hours, which brought the
head of our division to Bull Run and Sudley's Mill, where a halt of half an
hour took place, to rest and refresh the men and horses. From the heights
on this side of the run a vast column of the enemy could be plainly descried,
at the distance of a mile or more on our left, moving rapidly towards our*

line of march in front. Some disposition of skirmishers was then directed to be made at the head of the Column by the division commander, in which Colonel Slocum, of the Second Rhode Island Regiment, was observed to bear an active part. The column moved forward, however, before they were completed, and in about thirty minutes emerged from the timber, when the rattle of musketry and occasional crash of round shot through the leaves and branches of the trees in our vicinity betokened the opening of battle.

The head of the brigade was immediately turned slightly to the right, in order to gain time and room for deployment on the right of the Second Brigade. Griffin's battery found its way through the timber to the fields beyond, followed promptly by the marines, while the Twenty-seventh took direction more to the left, and the Fourteenth followed upon the trail of the battery, all moving up at a double-quick step. The enemy appeared drawn up in a long line, extending along the Warrenton turnpike from a house and haystacks upon our extreme right to a house beyond the left of the division. Behind that house there was a heavy masked battery, which, with three others along his line on the heights beyond, covered the ground upon which we were advancing with all sorts of projectiles. A grove in front of his right wing afforded it shelter and protection, while the shrubbery along the road, with fences, screened somewhat his left wing. Griffin advanced to within a thousand yards and opened a deadly and unerring fire upon his batteries, which were soon silenced or driven away. Our right was rapidly developed by the marines, Twenty-seventh, Fourteenth, and Eighth, with the cavalry in rear of the right, the enemy retreating with more precipitation than order as our line advanced.

The Second Brigade (Burnside's) was at this time attacking the enemy's right with, perhaps, too hasty vigor. The enemy clung to the protecting wood with great tenacity, and the Rhode Island Battery became so much endangered as to impel the commander of the Second Brigade to call for the assistance of the battalion of regulars. At this time I received the information through Capt. W. D. Whipple, A. A. G., that Colonel Hunter was seriously wounded, and had directed him to report to me as commander of the division; and in reply to the urgent request of Colonel Burnside, I detached the battalion of regulars to his assistance. For an account of its operations I would respectfully beg a reference to the enclosed report of its commander, Major Sykes [No. 35].

The rebels soon come flying from the woods towards the right, and the Twenty-seventh completed their rout by charging directly upon their center in the face of a scorching fire, while the Fourteenth and Eighth moved down the turnpike to cut off the retiring foe, and to support the Twenty-seventh, which had lost its gallant colonel, but was standing the brunt of the action, with its ranks thinning in the dreadful fire. Now the resistance of the enemy's left was so obstinate that the beaten right retired in safety.

The head of Heintzelman's column at this moment appeared upon the field, and the Eleventh and Fifth Massachusetts Regiments moved forward to the support of our center, while staff officers could be seen galloping rapidly in every direction, endeavoring to rally the broken Eighth; but this laudable purpose was only partially attained, owing to the inefficiency of some of its field officers.

The Fourteenth, though it had broken, was soon rallied in rear of Griffin's battery, which soon took up a position farther to the front and right, from which his fire was delivered with such precision and rapidity as to compel the batteries of the enemy to retire in consternation far behind the brow of the hill in front. At this time, my brigade occupied a line considerably in advance of that first occupied by the left wing of the enemy. The battery was pouring its withering fire into the batteries and columns of the enemy whenever they exposed themselves. The cavalry was engaged in feeling the left flank of the enemy's positions, in doing which some important captures were made--one by Sergeant Sacks, of the Second Dragoons, of a General George Steuart, of Baltimore. Our cavalry also emptied the saddles of a number of the mounted rebels.

General Tyler's division was engaged with the enemy's right. The Twenty-seventh was resting in the edge of the woods, in the center, covered by a hill, upon which lay the Eleventh and Fifth Massachusetts, occasionally delivering a scattering fire. The Fourteenth was moving to the right flank. The Eighth had lost its organization. The marines were moving up in fine style in rear of the Fourteenth, and Captain Arnold was occupying a height on the middle ground with his battery. At this juncture there was a temporary lull in the firing from the rebels, who appeared only occasionally on the heights in irregular formations, but to serve as marks for Griffin's guns.

The prestige of success had thus far attended the efforts of our inexperienced, but gallant, troops. The lines of the enemy had been forcibly shifted nearly a mile to their left and rear. The flags of eight regiments, though borne somewhat wearily, now pointed towards the hill from which disordered masses of rebels had been seen hastily retiring.

Griffin's and Ricketts' batteries were ordered by the commanding general to the top of the hill on our right, supporting them with Fire Zouaves and marines, while the Fourteenth entered the skirt of woods on their right, to protect that flank, and a column, composed of the Twenty-seventh New York, Eleventh and Fifth Massachusetts, First Minnesota, and Sixty ninth New York, moved up towards the left flank of the batteries; but so soon as they were in position, and before the flanking supports had reached theirs, a murderous fire of musketry and rifles, opened at pistol range, cut down every cannoneer and a large number of horses. The fire came from some infantry of the enemy, which had been mistaken for our own forces, an officer on the field having stated that it was a regiment sent by Colonel Heintzelman to support the batteries.

The evanescent courage of the zouaves prompted them to fire perhaps a hundred shots, when they broke and fled, leaving the batteries open to a charge of the enemy's cavalry, which took place immediately. The marines also, in spite of the exertions of their gallant officers, gave way in disorder; the Fourteenth on the right and the column on the left hesitatingly retired, with the exception of the Sixty-ninth and Thirty-eighth New York, who nobly stood and returned the fire of the enemy for fifteen minutes. Soon the slopes behind us were swarming with our retreating and disorganized forces, whilst rider less horses and artillery teams ran furiously through the flying crowd. All further efforts were futile; the words, gestures, and threats of our officers were thrown away upon men who had lost all presence of mind and only longed for absence of body. Some of our noblest and best officers lost their lives in trying to rally them.

Upon our first position the Twenty-seventh was the first to rally, under the command of Major Bartlett, and around it the other regiments engaged soon collected their scattered fragments. The battalion of regulars, in the meantime, moved steadily across the held from the left to the right, and took up a position where it held the entire forces of the rebels in check until our forces were somewhat rallied. The commanding general then ordered a retreat upon Centreville, at the same time directing me to cover it with the battalion of regulars, the cavalry, and a section of artillery. The rear guard thus organized followed our panic-stricken people to Centreville, resisting the attacks of the rebel cavalry and artillery, and saving them from the inevitable destruction which awaited them had not this body been interposed.

Among those who deserve especial mention I beg leave to place the following names, viz:

Captain Griffin, for his coolness and promptitude in action, and for the handsome manner in which he handled his battery. Lieutenant Ames, of the same battery, who, after being wounded, gallantly served with it in action, and being unable to ride on horseback, was helped on and off a caisson in changes of position.

Captain Tillinghast, A. Q. M., who was ever present where his services were needed, carrying orders, rallying troops, and serving with the batteries, and finally, I have to state with the deepest sorrow, was mortally wounded.

Major Sykes and the officers of his command, three of whom (Lieutenants Latimer, Dickinson, and Kent) were wounded, who by their discipline, steadiness, and heroic fortitude, gave éclat to our attacks upon the enemy, and averted the dangers of a final overthrow.

Major Palmer and the cavalry officers under him, who by their daring intrepidity made the effectiveness of that corps all that it could be upon such a field in supporting batteries, feeling the enemy's position, and covering our retreat.

Major Reynolds, Marines, whose zealous efforts were well sustained by his subordinates, two of whom, Brevet Major Zeilin and Lieutenant Hale, were wounded, and one, Lieutenant Hitchcock, lost his life.

Col. H. W. Slocum, who was wounded while leading his gallant Twenty-seventh New York to the charge, and Maj. J. J. Bartlett, who subsequently commanded it, and by his enthusiasm and valor kept it in action and out of the panic. His conduct was imitated by his subordinates, of whom two, Capt. H. C. Rodgers and Lieut. H. C. Jackson, were wounded, and one, Ensign Asa Park, was killed.

In the last attack Col. A.M. Wood, of the Fourteenth New York State Militia, was wounded, together with Captains R. B. Jordan and C. F. Baldwin, and Lieuts. J. A. Jones, T. R. Salter, R. A. Goodenough, and C. Scholes, and Adjutant Laidlaw.

The officers of the Fourteenth, especially Maj. James Jourdan, were distinguished by their display of spirit and efficiency throughout the action.

Surg. Charles C. Keeney, of the medical department, who by his professional skill, promptitude, and cheerfulness made the condition of the wounded of the Second Division comparatively comfortable. (He was assisted to a great extent by Dr. Rouch, of Chicago, a citizen.)

During the entire engagement I received extremely valuable aid and assistance from my aides-de-camp, Lieuts. C. F. Trowbridge and F. M. Bache, both of the Sixteenth Infantry.

Lieut. J. B. Howard, Fourteenth New York State Militia, A. A. Q. M. for the brigade, who by zealous attention to his duties succeeded in safely bringing the wagons of my brigade to Arlington.

The staff officers of the Second Division commander, via, Capt. W. D. Whipple, Lieutenants Cross and Flagler, served with me after the fall of Colonel Hunter, and I am indebted to them for gallant, faithful services during the day. Captain Whipple had his horse killed under him by a cannon ball.

Acting Asst. Adjt. General Lieut. W. W. Averell sustained the high reputation he had before won for himself as a brave and skillful officer, and to him I am very greatly indebted for aid and assistance, not only in performing with the greatest promptitude the duties of his position, but by exposing himself most fearlessly in rallying and leading forward the troops, he contributed largely to their general effectiveness against the enemy. I desire to call the attention of the commanding general particularly to him.

In conclusion, I beg leave to submit the enclosed return of killed, wounded, and missing in my brigade. Since the above reports were handed in many of the missing have returned, perhaps one-third of those reported. The enclosed report of Colonel Burnside, [No. 39], commanding Second Brigade, was sent to me after the above report was written. While respectfully calling the attention of the general commanding to it, I would also ask leave to notice some misconceptions under which the colonel commanding the Second Brigade seems to have labored at the time of writing his report, viz: Of his agency in the management or formation of the Second Division, on the field; 2d, of the time that his brigade was entirely out of the action, with the exception of the New Hampshire Regiment; 3d, of the position of his brigade in the retreat, and particularly of the position of the Seventy-first New York, as he may have mistaken the rear guard, organized under my direction by your orders, for the enemy.

Captain Arnold's battery and the cavalry were directed and placed in their positions by my senior staff officer up to the time when Colonel Heintzelman ordered the cavalry to the front of the column.

Very respectfully, your obedient servant,
A. PORTER,
Colonel Sixteenth Infantry, U. S. Army, Comdg

APPENDIX D

Report of Major George Sykes, 14th U.S. Infantry,

Commanding Battalion of Regulars

O.R.– SERIES I–VOLUME 2 [S# 2] — CHAPTER IX, pp. 390-391

HEADQUARTERS BATTALION OF REGULARS,

Camp Turnbull, Va., July 24, 1861

CAPTAIN: In compliance with your circular of the 23d instant, I have the honor to report the following casualties that occurred in my command during the recent battle before Manassas: Three commissioned officers wounded; one assistant surgeon missing; 13 rank and file killed, 17 wounded, 12 of whom are missing; 42 missing. A list is enclosed. Many of the latter are supposed to have taken the Alexandria road by mistake, and will no doubt rejoin their colors to-day.

This battalion, composed of two companies of Second U.S. Infantry, five companies of the Third U.S. Infantry, and one company of the Eighth Infantry, left its camp near Centreville about 3.30 a.m. on the 21st instant, and after a circuitous march of ten or twelve miles arrived on the enemy's left, and was immediately ordered to support the force under Colonel Burnside, which was suffering from a severe fire in its front. Our line was rapidly formed, opening fire, and a column under Colonel Heintzelman appearing at the same moment on our left, the enemy fell back to the rising ground in his rear. My battalion was then advanced to the front and took a position on the edge of a wood immediately opposite a masked battery and a large force of the secessionists posted about a house and the fences and trees around it. My three left companies were deployed as skirmishers under Captain Dodge, Eighth Infantry, and did great execution among their ranks. At this time the whole battalion became actively engaged, and a Rhode Island battery coming into action on my right, and having no support, at the request of its commanding officer, and seeing myself the necessity of the case, I remained as a protection to his guns. For more than an hour the command was here exposed to a concentrated fire from the batteries and regiments of the enemy, which seemed doubled when the guns of the Rhode Islanders opened. Many of my men assisted in working the latter battery.

As the attack of our Army became more developed on the right, and the necessity for my staying with the guns ceased, I moved my battalion in that direction, passing through crowds of retiring troops, whom we endeavored in vain to rally. Taking a position on the extreme right, in front of several regiments of the enemy, I opened an effective fire upon them, and held my ground until all our troops had fallen back and my flank was turned by a large force of horse and foot. I then retired a short distance in good order and facing to the enemy on the crest of a hill, held his cavalry in check, which still threatened our flank.

At this stage of the action, my command was the only opposing force to the enemy, and the last to leave the field. By taking advantage of woods and broken ground, I brought it off without loss, although the guns of our opponents were playing on our line of march from every height. While thus retiring, I received an order from the brigade commander to cover the retreat of that portion of the Army near me, which I did as well as I was able, remaining in rear until all of it had passed me.

After crossing Bull Run my command was threatened by a large force of cavalry, but its order and the regularity of its march forbade any attack. We reached our camp beyond Centreville at 8 p.m. It is but proper to mention that our officers and men were on their feet from 10 p.m. on the 20th until 10 a.m. on the 22d. Without rest, many without food, foot-sore, and greatly exhausted, they yet bore the retreat cheerfully, and set an example of constancy and discipline worthy of older and more experienced soldiers. My officers, nearly all of them just from civil life and the Military Academy, were eager and zealous, and to their efforts is due the soldierly retreat and safety of the battalion, as well as of many straggling volunteers who accompanied my command. The acting major, Capt. N. H. Davis, Second Infantry, rendered essential service by his coolness, zeal, and activity. Captain Dodge, Eighth Infantry, commanding the skirmishers on the left, was equally efficient, and to those gentlemen and all my officers I am indebted for cordial co-operation in all the movements of the day. Lieutenant Kent, although wounded, endeavored to retain command of his company, but a second wound forced him to give it up. He and Lieutenant Dickinson, acting adjutant, wounded, and Dr. Sternberg, U.S. Army, are believed to be in the hands of the enemy.

I beg to call the attention of the brigade commander to the services of Sergeant-Major Devoe, of the Third Infantry, who was conspicuous for his good conduct on the field. The arms and equipment of my command are in good condition, but the men are destitute of blankets, and in want of necessary clothing.

Very respectfully, your obedient servant,

GEORGE SYKES,

Major, Fourteenth Infantry, Commanding Battalion

Capt. W. W. AVERELL,

A. A. A. Gen., Porter's Brigade, Arlington, Va.

APPENDIX E

Casualties at First Manassas

<u>Killed officer</u> - 1

Second Lieutenant Hitchcock

<u>Killed privates</u> - 8

Privates Clegg, Harris, Hughes, Lane, Moore, Perkins, Riley, Ward.

<u>Wounded and absent corporal</u> -1

Corporal Steiner

<u>Wounded and absent privates</u> - 4

 Privates Stewart, Bowers, Slemons, Bradford.

<u>Wounded in the hospital</u> - 1 Major, 1 Second Lieutenant, 12 Privates

Brevet Major Zeilin, Lieutenant Hale (in quarters), Privates Dodge, Etchells, Tiger, Lang, McKenna, McCann, Whelan, McGuigan, Howell, Rannohan, Cook, Potter.

<u>Missing in Action</u> - 16 Privates

Privates Barrett, Hunt, McCristal, Clark, McCoy, Lewis, Beans, Dempsey, Kressler, Dermott, Otto, Cannon, Stanley, Ducanson, Foley, Wood.

Major Slack, quartermaster. Not in action.

<u>Total Strength</u> - 3 Majors; 1 Captain; 1 First Lt.; 6 2nd Lts.; 2 N.C. Staff; 4 First Sergeants; 3 2nd Sergeants; 8 Corporals; 2 Drummers; 2 fifers; 320 Privates; Aggregates: 353

44 killed, wounded, or missing in action; left for 'fit for duty' was: 309.

(US Navy Official Records of the Rebellion)

APPENDIX F

Uniforms and equipment of the Marine Battalion, July 1861

In 1859, just prior to the American Civil War, Commandant Henderson would die in office after serving 39 years as the Corps' senior officer. The new Commandant, John Harris, wanted to modernize the appearance of the Marine Corps and implemented a major uniform design change, which would closely follow European trends. American military fashion of the 1860s, would now be dominated by French styles, which was a historic departure from the British patterns that had governed American uniforms since the revolution. The 1859 designs would embrace these new fashion ideas while still incorporating several the Corps' earlier English influences. These new Marine uniforms would have a mix of the old and the new combining together to create a hybrid look that was characteristically American and has become distinctive to the era. The new uniform regulations would prescribe variations of the dark blue wool coat, and sky blue, or white linen in warm weather, trousers for all levels of uniform. This included fatigue, undress, and dress uniforms.

Marine "undress" uniforms; officer, first sergeant, and private (USMCHC)

The "undress" uniform, a new level of dress for the enlisted ranks, would fill the gap for general service and duty. The "dress" uniform, would now be reserved for more formal occasions, and "fatigue dress" would largely be confined to shipboard use. This new undress uniform, which would now become the principle field/combat uniform for the Marines, would still utilize the same bright colors of its dress counterpart. By today's standards, and with today's arms, it would seem quite foolish to go into combat in a bright colored uniform, with white belts and polished brass, but many of the intangibles we take for granted today as part of the Corps' ceremonies and traditions were in fact directly related to warfighting in those earlier eras. The concept of the squared away uniform, polished brass and boots, gleaming bayonets, and "snap and pop" in drill were often essential to the effectiveness and success in combat.

The weapons technology at the beginning of the Civil War would continue to dictate how battles were fought. The uniform would continue to play a vital role in the overall tactical strategy as a psychological tool. Having to stand in battle lines in remarkably proximity with their adversaries, the uniform was intended to impress, even intimidate the enemy. An ornate well-kept uniform projected a sense of discipline, esprit-de-corps, and professionalism.

The undress uniform consisted of a dark blue wool fatigue cap, or "kepi" of French pattern with a brass hunting horn infantry badge on the front. The badge contained a red leather backed solver "M" in its center. The officer's version of this fatigue cap was trimmed in black mohair cording and would be the first officers cap to officially bear a quatrefoil on it's top. The caps had an adjustable leather chin straps attached with two small marine buttons. Regulations prescribed that the straps were to be worn down when on duty, and up when off.

The enlisted undress coat was a single-breasted frock design of dark blue kersey wool. It had a stand up collar *"rising no higher than to permit the chin to turn freely over it,"* and welted in red at its base, where the collar joins the coat. There were seven large 1840 Marine buttons down the front, and two small Marine buttons on each cuff. Regulation called for the skirt of the coat was full cut, extending from the top of the hip to just below the crotch of the trousers. Images of the period show coat skirts of varying length. Since the skirt hem on the enlisted coat was issued "raw edged," the coats were initially issued with the skirt length roughly between the crotch and the knee allowing room for the skirt to be trimmed at the bottom. The coat had two large buttons in back along the seam where the skirt joins, marking where the waist belt rides. Non-commissioned officers wore rank chevrons on the upper sleeve. The style of chevrons was adopted in the 1850's and were similar in design to that of the U.S. Army. The chevrons were worn points up and made of half inch yellow silk taping with red cloth background. Two chevrons indicated a corporal, and three for a sergeant. Staff noncommissioned officers wore additions to chevrons such as a "lozenge," or diamond to indicate first sergeant. The drum major and quartermaster sergeant each wore three, flat bars below their chevrons. While the sergeant major wore three curved bars or "rockers" below their chevrons. Additionally, staff noncommissioned officers wore a red worsted sash around their waist to denote rank and billet. The officer's variation of the undress coat was dark blue wool, double breasted, without trim. Officer's rank was indicated by newly adopted "Russian Knots" worn on each shoulder.

Although the 1859 uniform regulations specify a shirt of dark blue wool flannel for normal wear, during hot weather an undyed muslin shirt was prescribed to be worn under the coat. A leather neck stock was prescribed for wear in garrison; however, it was often dispensed with in the field or at sea.

The service trousers were of sky-blue wool. Line officers and senior staff noncommissioned officers were authorized a narrow red welt down the outer seam of each trouser leg. During warm weather, plain white linen trousers were authorized for all ranks. This was the case of the Marines who participated in the campaign at Manassas.

Shoes were a standard smooth black leather military Jefferson Boot often referred to as "brogans." The belts were still of white buff leather, although the 1859 regulations called for the new "French" pattern equipment. This specified both the cartridge box and the bayonet to be worn on the waist belt. Evidence shows that the white cross belt continued in use for most of the Civil War. The exception to this was sergeants, who would now carry their accouterments on their belt. The officers wore a white glazed leather sword belt bearing an eagle and wreath buckle. They were also authorized to wear a black leather version of the sword belt with the undress uniform. It is believed that both variants were worn by Marine officers at Manassas.

On paper both the Army and the Marine Corps had accepted the 1855 rifled musket for use in the late 1850's. The M1855 did not go into production until 1857 with the Harpers Ferry and Springfield arsenals only turning out a small number in the years leading up to the outbreak of the Civil War. At the beginning of the war most Marines were still being issued the M1842 smoothbore musket to include the battalion of Marines that served at Manassas in July of 1861. Because the smoothbore muskets were slow to load and ineffective individually in both range and accuracy, tactics of the era would dictate massing these weapons together with Marines standing shoulder-to-shoulder allowing for a combined volume of fire. The "Marine Drill" and manual of arms being used at the beginning of the war had its origins dating back over two decades. Derived from "Scots Infantry Tactics" but modified for Marine Corps use and driven by the slow advancement in weapons technology, the base movements trace back to the American Revolution and the works of Baron von Steuben. The bayonet would also continue to be an intricate part of the musket and played both offensive and defensive rile in tactical doctrine.

In 1859 the Army pattern "Foot Officer's sword" was adopted by the Corps for both officers and noncommissioned officers, replacing both the officer's "mameluke" hilted sword, and the eagle head sergeant's sword. Marine officers would return to the Mameluke sword in 1868, but the Sergeants sword would stay in service and evolve into the current Marine NCO sword.

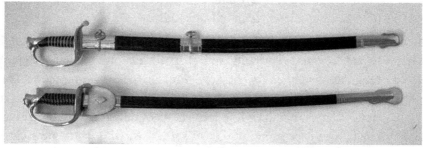

Marine officer and sergeant swords following the 1859 pattern (USMCHC)

Marine were normally issued packs and other equipment for service ashore. The Marine battalion at Manassas was mostly recruits and had only the barest of essentials available to them. No pack or tentage was issued and their only protection from the elements was their gray wool blanket and possibly a rubberized cloth "gum blanket" or an overcoat. Although requisitioned, there is no evidence to show that these latter two items arrived in time to be issued to the Marine Battalion prior to their march to Manassas. Lacking a pack, the Marines were instructed to form their blanket into a long roll, with the ends tied together, with a spare pair of socks inside. The blanket rolls were to be carried over the right shoulder during the march. All other logistical support equipment and supplies were to be provided through the U.S. Army Quartermaster system.

**Marine wearing blanket roll as prescribed
for the march to Manassas (USMCHC)**

Canteens and haversacks had to be emergency requisitioned. The canteen the Marines were issued was the same as that being used by the U.S. Army. Round, smooth-sided tin with a cork stopper. The cork canteen was commonly covered in a gray wool. The three-quarter inch wide strap was of natural oiled leather with an iron roller buckle for adjustment.

The haversack, used for carrying rations, was also the same as Army issue. Made of tarred canvas with sling, the bag was approximately 12 x 12 inches. Minimal rations consisted of hardtack, salted beef or pork, and some condiments such as coffee, salt and possibly sugar. A four-inch diameter tinned cup completed the Marines mess gear.

**Marine canteen, tinned cup, and
haversack with accoutrements (USMCHC)**

NOTES

[1] John W. Thomason, Jr., Captain, USMC, *JEB Stuart* (New York: Charles Scribner's Sons, 1934), 47.

[2] Bernard C. Nalty, *United States Marines at Harpers Ferry and in the Civil War* (Washington, DC: Historical Division, Headquarters, U.S. Marine Corps, 1983), 1-4.

[3] Ibid.

[4] American Battlefield Trust, John Brown Biography, 2009.

[5] Fergus M. Bordewich, "John Brown's Day of Reckoning," *Smithsonian Magazine*, October 2009.

[6] David M. Sullivan, *The United States Marines in the Civil War* – Volume 1 (Shippensburg, PA: Beidel Printing House).

[7] Reynolds was not a graduate of the United States Military Academy. He was dismissed during his senior year.

[8] Robert E. Hitchcock to "My Dear Mother," U.S. Marine Barrack, July 5, 1861. Hitchcock Pp. MCHC.

[9] John E. Reily to "Dear Mother and Father," Marine Barracks [sic], Washington D.C. July 10 (1861). Pension application of James Reily Certificate 2821. National Archives

[10] Andrew Porter (1820-1872). Non-graduate, U.S. Military Academy. Appointed First Lieutenant in 1846. Breveted twice for gallantry during the Mexican War. Promoted through the grades to the rank of Brigadier General, August 6, 1861. Resigned, April 20, 1864.

[11] Ramsay's information, even to the brigade the Marine battalion would be attached to, was accurate. Ramsay to Harris, U.S. Sloop *Richmond*, New York, July 11, 1861. RG 127, Letters Received -HD.

[12] Harris to Ramsay, Headquarters, Jul 13, 1861. RG 127 Letters Sent.

[13] Telegram. Welles to Ramsay, Navy Department, July 13, 1861. Copy in RG 127, Letters Sent.

[14] Irvin McDowell (1818-1885), U. S. Military Academy, Class of 1838. Breveted Captain for gallantry during the Mexican War. Promoted through the grades to the rank of Brigadier General, May 14, 1861. Promoted to Major General, November 25, 1872. Retired, 1882.

[15] Cameron to Welles.

[16] Telegram. Welles to Reynolds, Navy Department, July 13, 1861. Copy to RG 127, Letters Sent. Reynolds had been ordered from Marine Barracks, Boston, on personal matters, and was in that city when orders were sent from the Navy Department, Telegram, Welles to Zeilen, Navy Department, July 14, 1861. Copy in RG 127, Letters Sent.

[17] Welles to Harris, Navy Department, July 15, 1861. RG 80, Letters to Marine Officers.

[18] Cartter to "Dear Mother," Washington, July 14, 1861. Cartter Family Papers, Manuscripts Division, Library of Congress.
[19] Hitchcock Pp. MCHC

[20] As quoted in Stephen B. Oates, *With Malice Toward None: The Life of Abraham Lincoln* (New York, 1977), 271.

[21] RG 127, Letters Received -HD

[22] Telegram. Slack to Maddox, Washington, July 15, 1861. RG 127 Letters Sent QM.

[22] S. H. Huntington to "My Dear Wife," Washington, July 14, 1961. RG 127 Letters Sent QM.

[24] Harris to Wells, Headquarters, 16 July 1861. RG 80, Letters from Marine Officers, Pennypacker, who enlisted at Philadelphia on June 5, 1861, and was discharged on July 20, 1861.

[25] Edward K. Eckert and Nicholas J. Amato, eds. *Ten Years in the Saddle: The Memoir of William Woods Averell* (San Rafael, CA. 1978), 290.

[26] Ibid.

[27] David Hunter (1802-1886). U. S. Military Academy, Class of 1822. Resigned, 1836. Appointed paymaster and Major, March 14, 1842. Appointed Colonel, May 14, 1861, Brigadier General of Volunteers to rank from May 17, 1861, and Major General of Volunteers to rank, from August 13, 1861. Presided over the military trial of the Lincoln Assassination Conspirators.

[28] Henry Warner Slocum (1827-1894). U. S. Military Academy, Class of 1852.
    George Sykes (1822-1880). U. S. Military Academy, Class of 1842.
    Innis Newton Palmer (1824-1900). U.S. Military Academy, Class of 1864.
    Charles Griffin (1825-1867). U.S. Military Academy, Class of 1847.

[29] O.R. 2:304

[30] C. B. Fairchild, ed. *History of the 27th Regiment N.Y.* (Binghamton, N.Y. 1888), 10.

[31] Col. Daingerfield Parker, USA, "Personal Reminiscences: The Battalion of Regular Infantry at the First Battle of Bull Run," Military Order of the Loyal Legion of the United States, Commandery of the District of Columbia, War Papers (Washington, 1899), 7.

[32] Captain Robert G. Carter, USA, (Ret) Four Brother in Blue or Sunshine and Shadows of the War of the Rebellion. A story of the Great Civil War from Bull Run to Appomattox. (Reprint of the 1913 Edition, Austin, 1978), 11.

[33] The severity of the day resulted in troops collapsing from the heat. Pvt. Robert Galbraith of Company B fell out of the line of march and lapsed into

unconsciousness by the side of the road from the effects of the sun. He was revived by an Army teamster, taken to the camp of the Marine Battalion at Spring Hill Farm, and recovered sufficiently to take part in the Battle of Bull Run two days later. Pension Application of Robert Galbraith, National Archives.

[34] O.R. 2:307.

35 Cartter Pp., L.C.

[36] The U. S. Infantry Battalion was commanded by Major George Sykes.

[37] This was the last instance of enlisted men being made to suffer the lash as punishment in the military service of the Unites States.

[38] Hitchcock Pp. MCHC

[39] 11 Daniel Tyler (1799-1882). U. S. Military Academy, Class of 1819. Resigned in 1834. Appointed Colonel, 1st Connecticut Volunteers and Brigadier General of Volunteers at the outbreak of the war. Mustered out on August 11, 1861, but reappointed Brigadier General of Volunteers, August 13, 1861. Resigned April 6, 1864.

[40] O.R. 2:326-327.

[41] Alton *(Illinois) Evening Democrat*, Tuesday evening, July 30, 1861, "Two Alton Boys in the Battle of Bull's Run."

[42] Quote taken from an undated clipping from an unidentified Vermont newspaper found in the Hitchcock personal papers (Pp), MCHC.

[43] Ambrose Everett Burnside (1824-1881). U. S. Military Academy, Class of 1847. Appointed Colonel, 1st Rhode Island Volunteers at the start of the war. Appointed Brigadier General of Volunteers, August 9, 1861, and Major General of Volunteers, March 18, 1862. Commanding General, Army of the Potomac, November 1862-March 1863. Resigned, April 15, 1865.

[44] John P. Victory to "The Editor of the Brooklyn Eagle," Headquarters, 14th Regiment N.Y.S.M. July 25, 1861. *Brooklyn Daily Eagle*, July 31st, 1861, p.1.

[45] William Woods Averell (1832-1900). U.S. Military Academy, Class of 1855. Appointed Brigadier General of Volunteers, September 26, 1862. Breveted Brigadier and Major General, U.S. Army, at the close of the war. Resigned, May 18, 1865.

[46] Eckert and Amato, *Ten Years in the Saddle*, 295.

[47] Pierre Gustave Toutant Beauregard (1818-1893), U. S. Military Academy, Class of 1838. Breveted twice for gallantry during the Mexican War. Resigned his commission as Captain of Engineers, February 1861. Appointed Brigadier General, PACS, March 1, 1861. Promoted to General, Confederate Army to rank from July 21, 1861. Paroled at Greensboro, NC, April 26, 1865.

[48] Major Augustus S. Nicholson, adjutant of the Marine Battalion, was convinced that a Virginian named Machen, whose house was on the line of the flank march, rode to the Confederate lines to alert General Beauregard to the danger. No evidence of Nicholson's allegation has ever been uncovered. Carter, *Four Brothers in Blue*, 27.

[49] Edward Porter Alexander, (1835-1910), U. S. Military Academy, Class of 1857. Resigned, May 1, 1861. Appointed Captain of Engineers, PACS, February 26, 1864. Surrendered at Appomattox Court House, April 9, 1865.

[50] Gary W. Gallegher, ed., *Fighting for the Confederacy: The Personal Recollections of General Edward Porter Alexander* (Chapel Hill, 1989), 50.

[51] Nathan George Evans (1824-1868), U.S. Military Academy, Class of 1848. Resigned, February 1861. Appointed colonel, 4th South Carolina. Promoted Brigadier General, PACS, October 21, 1861.

[52] Barnard Elliot Bee (1824-1861). U. S. Military Academy, Class of 1845. Breveted to 1st Lt. and Captain for gallantry during the Mexican War. Resigned his captain's commission on March 3, 1861. Appointed Lieutenant Colonel, 1st South Carolina Regulars, on June 1, 1861, and Brigadier General, PACS, on June 17, 1861. Killed in action at Bull Run, July 21, 1861.

li S. H. Huntington to "My Dear Wife," Washington, July 21, 1861. Huntington Pp., MCHD

[53] James Brewerton Ricketts (1817-1887). U. S. Military Academy, Class of 1839. Promoted through the grades to the rank of Brigadier General of Volunteers to rank from July 21, 1861. Breveted Major General of Volunteers, August 1, 1864, and of the Regular Army, March 13, 1865. Retired, January 3, 1867.

[54] John Daniel Imboden (11823-1895). Elected Captain, Staunton Artillery, April 1861. Organized the 1st Virginia Partisan Rangers and appointed its Colonel, summer 1862. Promoted to Brigadier General, PACS, January 28, 1863.

[55] Imboden viewed the matter differently. He reported that he kept up the duel with Griffin and Ricketts from his position on Henry Hill until he was compelled to withdraw for lack of infantry support. In fact, Imboden claimed to have been the only opposition to the Federal advance for more than a half hour after the Confederate troops retreated from the battlefield north of the Warrenton Turnpike. John D. Imboden, "Incidents of the First Bull Run," *Battles and Leaders of the Civil War*, 4 vols., New York: Century, 1887, I, 229-239.

[56] *Pittsburgh Post,* July 31, 1861. "Letter From a Marine Who was at Bull's Run." The writer was identified only as "W. B." at the end of the item. He was, in fact, William Barrett, who enlisted in the Marine Corps at Pittsburgh on June 13, 1861. My thanks to Mike Kane of Pittsburgh, who brought this item to my attention.

[57] Baker letter, *Alton Evening Democrat.*

[58] O.R. 2:383.

[59] S. H. Huntington to "My Dear Wife," Washington, July 25, 1861, relating a conversation with Captain Jones, following the battle. Huntington Pp., MCHD.

[60] William Farquhar Barry (1818-1879). U.S. Military Academy, Class of 1838. Appointed through the grades to the rank of Brigadier General of Volunteers, August 20, 1861, and to Major General of Volunteers and Regulars during the course of the war. Reverted to the rank of Colonel at the end of the war.

[61] "Report of the Joint Committee on the Conduct of the War: The Battle of Bull Run." The Reports Committee of the Senate of the United States for the Third Session on the Congress in Four Volumes (Washington, 1863). 2: 168-169. Testimony of Captain Charles Griffin, January 4, 1862.

[62] O.R., 2:383.

[63] Testimony of William W. Averell, January 28, 1862. "Joint Committee on the Conduct of the War," 2: 215

[64] Ibid., 216.

[65] Edward S. Dana to "Dear Sir," Washington D.C., August 1, 1861. Letter to Dr. William Hitchcock, Lieutenant Hitchcock's father, in the Hitchcock Pp., MCHD.

[66] Baker Letter, *Alton Evening Democrat.*

[67] Griffin's Testimony, "Joint Committee on the Conduct of the War," 2: 169. Major Barry's testimony before the Committee showed evidence of selective memory. He denied ever giving Griffin orders not to fire on the regiment, although he admitted he thought the troops were the 14th Brooklyn. Ibid, 142-149.

[68] Barrett Letter, *Pittsburgh Post.* Francis Harris enlisted in the Marine Corps at Pittsburgh, June 8, 1861.

[69] The combination of the haphazard and desultory firing of the Zouaves and Marines and the volleys of the 14th Brooklyn took a heavy toll among the 33rd Virginia. Forty-three were killed and one hundred and forty were wounded. "Colonel Cummings' Account," *Southern Historical Society Papers*, 34, 1906, 367-371.

[70] Griffin's Testimony, "Joint Committee of the Conduct of the War," 2: 169.

[71] Charles Tevis, "*Colonel Fowler's Own Story,*" *The History of the Fighting Fourteenth* (New York, 1911), 230. See also, Robert Hunt Rhodes, ed., *All for the Union: A History of the 2nd Rhode Island Volunteer Infantry in the War of the Great Rebellion, As told by the diary and letters of Elisha Hunt Rhodes, who enlisted as a private in '61 and rose to command of his regiment* (Lincoln, R.I., 1985), 34. Rhodes reported leaving his regiment and going forward to see what was happening on Henry Hill. He came upon a spot where the trees were spattered with blood and the ground covered by the bodies of Marines and Louisiana Zouaves. Since Louisiana Zouave Battalion had been severely battered during earlier fighting on Matthews's Hill, it had left the field and was not engaged on Henry Hill. To what regiment these dead Zouaves belonged remains a mystery.

---

[72] Ibid.

[73] D(anile). B. Conrad, "History of the First Battle of Manassas and the Organization of the Stonewall Brigade," *Southern Historical Society Papers* (Richmond, 1891) Vol. 19, 82-94. In 1883, Lt. Col. E. B. Fowler, commanding officer of the 14th Brooklyn, stated that the Marines broke and ran after receiving the volley from Jackson's troops, and were followed by the "unsupported Fourteenth." However, Conrad's personal observations of the bodies lying on the ground in and near the Confederate position cast serious doubt on Fowler's statement. It is possible that Fowler's comments were embellishments of the 14th's combat reputation at Bull Run, while Conrad had nothing to gain by reporting that the corpses of Marines lay beyond those from the Brooklyn regiment.

[74] William Owen Miller, *In Camp and Battle with the Washington Artillery of New Orleans* (Boston, 1885), 41. Andrew Douglas Ramsay was an unsuccessful applicant for a Marine Corps commission in early March 1847 despite personal recommendations from both President James K. Polk and Secretary of the Navy John Y. Mason. He was subsequently appointed a second lieutenant of the 1st Artillery Regiment to rank from 7 June 1855 and promoted to first lieutenant in February 1861. An account of Ramsay's death may be found in C.A. Fonerden, *Military History of Carpenter's Battery* (New Market, 1911), 10-11. Ramsay's corpse was stripped its fine garments, with the exception of the silk stockings, by an unknown rebel after the battle.

[75] This attack may have been launched in support of the 69th New York. The New Yorkers spearheaded the last attempt to retake Henry Hill from the Dudley Road position. Pvt. William Barrett stated, "We were the first called to assist the 69th."

[76] S. H. Huntington to "My Dear Wife," Washington, 25 July 1861. Huntington Pp. MCHC.

[77] Oliver Otis Howard (1830-1909). U. S. Military Academy, Class of 1854. Elected Colonel. 5th Maine Volunteers, May 5, 1861. Resigned his Regular Army commission, June 7, 1861. Brigadier General of Volunteers, September 3, 1861.Major General of Volunteers, November 29, 1862. Re-appointed to the Regular Army, with rank of Brigadier General, December 21, 1864. Promoted Major General, 1886. Retired, 1894.

[78] Arnold Elzey (1816-1871). U. S. Military Academy, Class of 1837. Breveted for gallantry during the Mexican War. Resigned his captain's commission on April 25, 1861. Appointed Colonel, 1st Maryland Infantry, April-May 1861. Appointed Brigadier General PACS, to rank from July 21, 1861. Promoted to Major General, December 1861. Appointed, Brigadier General, PACS, October 9, 1862, and to General, PACS, February 19, 1864. Commanding General, Trans-Mississippi Department, January 1863-June 1865. Surrendered at Galveston, Texas, June 2, 1865.

[79] S. H. Huntington to "My Dear Wife," Washington, July 25, 1861. Huntington Pp., MCHC.

[80] Hitchcock's body was never recovered from the battlefield. It was undoubtedly buried in one of the mass graves dug by the Confederates in the days following the battle. A memorial service was held for 2nd Lt. Hitchcock at Shoreham, Vermont, his hometown, on September 11, 1861.

[81] Baker Letter, *Alton Evening Democrat.*

[82] Barrett Letter, *Pittsburgh Post.*

[83] Daniel Quinn to Jacob Zeilen, Charlestown, MA., October 28, 1868. RG 127, Letters received. HD.

[84] Eckert S. Barrett, "Adventures at Bull Run," Frank Moore, ed., *The Civil War in Song and Story, 1860-1865.* (P. G. F. Collier, Pub., n.p. 1889) 256-261.

[85] O.R. 2:390-391

[86] S. H. Huntington to "My Dear Wife," Washington, July 24, 1861. Huntington Pp. MCHC

[87] Harris to Welles, Headquarters, July 26, 1861. RG 80 Letters from Marine Officers.

[88] Welles to Cameron, Navy Department, July 24, 1861. Copy in RG 127, Letters Received-HD

[89] Cartter Pp., LC.

[90] Private Stanley was originally listed as "Missing." In Major Reynolds' after-action report, See N.O.R., 4:581. Stanley's family was still trying to find out what happened to him as late as April 1862. See Jonas White to" The Hon. Col. John Harris, Comm'ant. Of Marine Corps at Washington City," Philadelphia, April 28, 1862. Letters Received – GR.

[91] RG 127, Letters Sent.

[92] Perkins had suffered a gunshot wound through the left ankle and had been left on the battlefield. He was exchanged on January 5, 1862 and restored to duty. He died in Camden NJ, November 17, 1919. Pension Certificate 2378.

[93] Harris to Miss Mary Barrett, Headquarters, July 29, 1861. RG 127. Letters Received GR. It is assumed that all response letters informing loved ones that a son, husband or brother was missing or had been killed in action were very similar.

[94] N.O.R., 4:581. "[Subclosure.] Report of Marine Battalion under the command of Major John G. Reynolds in the recent battle before Manassas, July 21, 1861," submitted by Aug. S. Nicholson, Adjutant and Inspector, Marine Barracks, Washington, D.C., July 21, 1861. This list of killed, wounded, and missing does not appear with Reynolds' report as printed in O.R., 2:391-392.

[95] Henry Clark's father was employed by the Canada Powder Company of Hamilton, Ontario, Canada, and very concerned about the fate of his son. Three letters written between August 5-23, 1861, can be found in RG 127, Letters Received, HD. Jno H.P. White to "The Hon Gideon Welles," Acton, Massachusetts, August 29, 1861, and Lewis Wood to "Hon. Gideon Welles, Winslow, New Jersey, April 4, 1862. RG 127, Letters Received-GR, Mrs. Sarah Hamm to "the Hon. Col. Harris," Philadelphia, August 5, 1861, and May 28, 1861, RG 127, Letters Received GR. Pension Certificate 560, National Archives, in the name of Honora Barrett, mother of Private John Barrett. Upon his return from rebel hands, Barrett was posted to duty at Marine Barracks, Philadelphia. Surg. James M. Greene, USN, reported that Private Barrett was frequently unable to perform his duties due to chronic debility. Surgeon Greene recommended that the ailing Marine be released from the service on February 6, 1862. Barrett was discharged on Surgeon's Certificate for consumption, on February 6, 1862. He died of the disease on May 5, 1862. Stewart served in Company C, 10th U.S. Infantry, April 3, 1856-April 3, 1861, and enlisted in the Marine Corps on June

17, 1861. Pension Certificate of William Stewart, 16216, National Archives. John Cannon to Harris, Philadelphia, July 29, 31, and August 1861, RG 127, Letters Received-HD. Michael Cannon to Harris, Philadelphia, June 12 and July 15, 1862, RG 127, Letters Received-GR. Pension Certificate of Robert Duncanson, 19203, National Archives.

[96] N.O.R. 4:581 (Subenclosure).

[97] RG 127, Muster Rolls Muster roll for Headquarters, July 1861.

[98] Pension Certificate of Garrett Steiner, 13589, National Archives.

[99] Corporal Steiner and Private Stewart, Otto, Perkins, and Barrett joined Liggon's as soon as they were sufficiently recovered from their wounds.

[100] William H. Jeffery, *Richmond Prisons*, 1861-1862. (St. Johnsbury, VT., 1893), 8.

[101] Benjamin F. Perkins joined at Headquarters, January 5, 1862, John Barrett, January 8, Robert Duncanson, January 15, William Stewart, January 19, and Frederick Otto, February 23, 1862. RG 127, Muster Rolls. Muster Rolls of Headquarters, January, and February 1862. It is interesting to note that when Perkins and Stewart applied for payment in lieu of the rations they were entitles to while prisoners of war, the 4th Auditor demanded proof of their captivity. See, Hobart Berrian, 4th Auditor to Major William Russell, Paymaster, Washington March 24, 1862.

[102] The Pension Applications of Jacob Kressler, Navy 4500, and Abel J. Wood, Navy 20364, both describe the miserable conditions during their confinement at New Orleans.

[103] David Glasgow Farragut (1801-1870). Appointed midshipman, December 17, 1810.Promoted through the grades to the ranks of Rear Admiral, July 16, 1862, Vice Admiral, December 31, 1864, and Admiral, July 26, 1866.

[104] Jeffery, *Richmond Prisons*, 148.

[105] Ibid., 149.

---

[106] Garland to Harris, Brooklyn, June 3, 4, 13 and 14, 1862. RG 127, Letters Received HD.

[107] Margaret Leech, Reveille in Washington, 1860-1865(New York, 1941), 106. RG 127 Letters Sent.

[108] The flag was sent to Philadelphia for repair, and replacement of the staff and tassels which were left on the battlefield during the retreat. S. H. Marks, Quartermaster's August 14, 1861. RG 127 QM Letters Sent.

[109] RG 127, Letters Received-HD

[110] RG 127, Letters Received-GR

BIBLIOGRAPHY

Carter, Robert G., *Four Brothers in Blue or Sunshine and Shadows of the War of the Rebellion*. Austin, 1978

Collum, Robert S., Major, *The History of the United States Marine Corps*. New York, 1902.

Connelly, William Elsey. *John Brown*. Topeka: Crane & Company, 1900.

Donnelly, Ralph W. *Biographical Sketches of the Commissioned Officers of the Confederate States Marine Corps*. Washington, NC, 1983.

Drew, Thomas. *The John Brown Invasion: An Authentic History of the Harpers Ferry Tragedy*. Boston, 1860.

Eckert, Edward K., and Nicholas J. Amato. Eds. *Ten Years in the Saddle: The Memoir of William Woods Averell*. San Rafael, CA., 1978

Hinton, Richard J. *John Brown and His Men*. New York: Funk & Wagnalls, 1894; Reprint New York: Arno, 1968.

McClellan, Maj. H. B., *The Life, Character and Campaigns of Major-Gen. J.E.B. Stuart*, Richmond, VA., 1860.

Moore, Rayburn S., "John Brown's Raid at Harpers Ferry: An Eyewitness Account by Charles White," Virginia Magazine of History and Biography. October 1959. 387-395.

Muehlbauer, Matthew S. and David J. Ulbrich. *Ways of War*; 2nd Ed. New York: Routledge, 2018.

Nalty, Bernard, C. *United States Marines at Harpers Ferry and in the Civil War*. History and Museums Division, Headquarters, US Marine Corps, Washington DC. 1983.

Oates, Stephen B. *To Purge this Land with Blood: A Biography of John Brown*. New York: Harper & Row, 1970.

Parker, Dangerfield, "Personal Reminiscences: The Battalion of Regular Infantry at the First Battle of Bull Run." *Military Order of the Loyal Legion of the United States, Commandery of the District of Columbia War Papers*. Washington, 1899.

Sanborn, F. B. *Memoirs of John Brown*. Concord, 1878.

Sanborn, F. B., ed. *Life and Letters of John Brown*. Boston: Roberts Brothers, 1885.

Sullivan, David M. *The United States Marines in the Civil War; The First Year*. (Shippensburg, PA: White Mane Publishing Company, 1997).

Villard, Oswald Garrison. *John Brown, 1800-1859: A Biography Fifty Years After*. Gloucester, MA: Peter Smith, 1965.

INDEX

CPSIA information can be obtained
at www.ICGtesting.com
Printed in the USA
JSHW051554270122
22337JS00007B/159